BAD GIRL
VIRTUOUS WOMEN

Janet Evans

2021

Bad Girl
VIRTUOUS WOMAN

Copyright © 2021 Janet Evans

ISBN 978-1-946683-36-6
Library of Congress Control Number 2021912406
Published by
Rapier Publishing Company
Dothan, Alabama 36301
www.rapierpublishing.com
Facebook: www.rapierpublishing@gmail.com
Twitter: rapierpublishing@rapierpub

Printed in the United States of America
All rights reserved under the International Copyright Law.
Contents and/or cover may not be reproduced in whole or in part in any form without the consent of the Publisher, or Author.

Book Cover Design: Garrett Myers
Book Layout: Rapture Graphics

This story is based on and inspired by true events. The characters depicted in this work are solely those of the author and do not reflect the publisher; therefore, the publisher hereby disclaims any responsibility for them.

BAD GIRL VIRTUOUS WOMAN

This book is designed to let the readers see that we can always obtain a better place in life. I believe we all start off wanting to be or stay "a good girl." After all, isn't that what we were encouraged to be from the time when we first understood what approval was? When we first stood up holding onto the arm of the chair, we were applauded "that's a good girl." Then with our first steps, we were told, "That's a good girl." Even when we fell down, we were told, "It's ok, get up, you can do it! "That's a good girl." This book will tell how a good girl fell into a bad girl role and rose up to be a virtuous woman. Your destiny is glorious, even if it doesn't look that way right now. There is a saying, and that is, "What doesn't kill you will make you stronger.

Life happens to us all and it's filled with swift transitions. One day you are a child unassuming and carefree then life happens. Finding your way through life's transitions can lead to roads that without a roadmap or GPS (God's Precious Son) could cause death and destruction. In life we need to discern which roads to take and the people that we encounter on those roads.

Fun and excitement can be had on our journey. But what we may not be ready for is when those traveling with us unexpectedly have their journey's end. My question was, why did I survive?
The answer led me to the life I live and it's still full of fun and excitement. But now it's s the road to life that is more abundantly.

Chapter 1

I Believed - Good Girl

(Hey, Hey, Don"t be Trying to Skip to the Bad Girl Chapter)

See how our nature to experience the "Bad Girl" is at work in our flesh at all times. Paul says in Romans 7:17, "I am at war within myself to do good or bad." A kindergartener in a Christian School who attends both Sunday School and Vacation Bible School can formulate a strong faith, so much so that the child's relationship with the Savior is even closer than that of the parents who birth him or her. Case and point, Jesus's relationship with God the Father led him to the temple, where he, at age 12, is in the midst of the teachers, listening and asking questions that amazed even them that were teachers of the law. After a full day's journey, Jesus's parents finally found him and asked him why he disappeared. His response was quite baffling. He replied, "Did you not know I must be about my Father's business." Loving and obeying God, the Father was a part of him that even his natural parents didn't quite understand. So, it was with me, the loving God that I believed in was real to me, even at the age of 6. I talked to him about my problems.

Well, I'm sure you're thinking what problems a six-year-old could possibly have, one that seemed big enough to me that I needed Jesus to get me out of. My best friend always went to Chicago during summer vacation to visit her aunt. She would always come back with beautiful clothing, hair bows, and stories of the great fun she had. I missed her and was glad to see her when she returned. The One thing I couldn't understand was why I was always starting a fight with her over nothing. Then Jesus showed me the problem was not my friend but me. I was jealous of her and the things she would receive from her aunt. So, the Sunday school lesson about Joseph and his coat that his brothers hated him for (Genesis 37 3:4) was not for someone else but for me. What would I do? Stay jealous and start fights that would cause me not to have my friend to play with or confess to Jesus my sin? Jesus was also my friend and heaven knows with my attitude I needed him to be my friend. I was taught He'd help in the time of trouble and never leave me, although he couldn't play paper dolls, hopscotch, or hide and go seek with me when my friend was in Chicago. I had to do what I was hearing the choir sing about on Sunday: Have a little talk with Jesus.

    So, after having a big blow up with my friend Karen and making it across the street from her house to our apartment, I stood at the corner of the apartment crying because God showed me my sin. But yet, I was still doing the same thing each time we played. I didn't feel good about the whole deal. I said to Jesus, "Lord, I know it's me. Please forgive me and take the jealousy away so that I can get along with my friend." Without a moment's hesitation, His presence just walked up on me, reassuring me that He had heard me and answered my prayer. From that moment on, jealousy was no longer a problem. I was happy again, and anytime someone had something more beautiful than mine, I was still happy. Now my faith in my unseen friend was even more real and the reason I was always ready to go to church even when my parents weren't.

Janet Evans

Then there was that other friend, the one that was thrust upon you. You know the brother that sticks closer than a friend? I really never got much of a chance to call him my little brother because we were what some people call Irish Twins- 11 months apart. For one month each year, we were both the same age. Since "big sister, little brother" wasn't an issue, what was it we fought about so much? I still haven't figured that one out. Mom and Dad with Jan and Rickey, we were the perfect little family, the handsome couple and their two children. My dad was the tall, dark and handsome, well-dressed, convertible-new-car-driving guy, and my mom was the well-built, smart cutie with a tenacious streak. Both maturing into adulthood during the era of James Brown's "This is a Man's World" and Martin Luther King Jr.'s "I Have a Dream." A time when the "Black Man" no longer feared the white man's lynching or saying "yes sir" to a boy the age of his youngest son. The time when my mother was no longer just cleaning the white woman's house or taking care of her children. Now, she has the dream and tenacity to go to school and get a job in nursing, move from that apartment, and buy us a home of our own. Yes, buy a house for Jan and Rickey.

Chapter 2

A House Is Not A Home

My mom finished her nursing classes, stopped cleaning houses and taking care of the rich, over the mountain socialite kids. She and my dad, the construction worker, were ready to move on up. Daddy was out of town working for a big, well-established, construction company out of Birmingham, Alabama. He traveled to the Midwest a lot. That was fine with us. After all, the new house called for sacrifices. Besides, my parents were not strangers to hard work. They had come a long way from where they'd started from in Talladega County, Alabama.

I remembered my mom saying how she had picked cotton for her Uncle George, who I remember vividly, as my great-grandmother LeGulia's brother. He owned a lot of land and sold my great-grandmother a small place down in the woods. As a child, I thought he was the meanest man on earth. There was every type of fruit tree on his land, but Uncle George didn't want any of us to touch them, not even one apple. It was the place you loved to hate because as part of the sacrifice for the new house, Rickey and I were sent to stay down in the country. Mom would go spend time in Indiana with my Dad where he was working.

It was hard for us to give up our big city ways to come to

Janet Evans

a farm with chickens clucking around the yards and even one time around Rickey's behind. He was stooping behind the house in the woods using the "bathroom," which was something else they didn't have at great-grandma LeGulia's (another sacrifice). I don't know why he wasn't using the outhouse. Perhaps one of the other barnyard animals was already occupying the facility. When Rickey came from behind the house screaming and pulling up his pants with a chicken flying behind him, we were both ready to head back to Birmingham.

There were good times as well. Of course, not being able to watch TV and only being able to listen to country western on the radio were not among them. Walking a country mile to get to our cousin's house was great because on the way we got to walk across a spring using a big tree limb as a bridge. We got to eat off trees along the way. Looking back now, we probably could have jumped across that spring without getting too wet, much less drowning. Those really were the best of times, when dreams of the future were as pure as that clear spring that ran behind great-grandma LeGulia's house.

Oh, if I could turn back the hands of time! As a matter of fact, that was the song my Dad was singing to my mom about this time. He had done an awful thing which I believe was the beginning of our house no longer being a home. After the sacrifices made by my mother to purchase a house of our own, my dad came home driving a new car bought with money that was supposed to go towards the down payment of the new house. On that day, I wish that I had known the Lord like Joshua (Joshua 10:12-13). I too would have prayed that the sun and moon stood still, at least until Daddy decided not to leave that car lot with that car.
Well, that was really a setback, but they fought through that.

Maggie, my mom, being as tenacious as she was, wasn't about to allow that to stop her from the dream, but I think it did greatly diminish the dream of them accomplishing it together. Mom had decided she would be able to do it by herself and that she could do bad all by herself. Dad saw the error of his ways and started singing a new song, "Ain't Too Proud to Beg," by the Temptations. We heard that song playing not only on a wax "45 record," but with a couple of drinks of scotch. The theatrics were on, the tears would flow, and the begging on bended knees like the Temp's did on stage was something to see. The only part of "It's a Man's World" we were hearing from then on was, "a man ain't nothing without a woman or a girl." For about the next three years, we remained in the apartment. We moved from the one bedroom on the front street to the two-bedroom apartment on the back row.

Chapter 3

A New Face of Jesus

During this time, we attended Lively Hope Baptist Church —we being my mom, my brother and I. My dad attended Peace Baptist. I would visit Peace Baptist where dad sometimes attended because my best friend went there too. Mom refused to go there for some reason —something to do with the fellowship dad and some sister at that church had. I didn't understand because my dad only had one sister and she lived in New Jersey. Anyway, the "Spirit of Peace" from that church never followed my dad home. Now Lively Hope Baptist Church wasn't a place that I remember people really rejoicing and praising the Lord. Except when someone occasionally crying out and an usher board member running to them in their white uniform and a little hat with a fan and some smelling salts if they passed out. I really enjoyed learning about Jesus at Sunday school; the things they taught were so real to me. I was totally convinced of the Savior being who the Sunday school books said He was. I wanted to be baptized —yes take me to the water. I do remember my mom getting our things ready for that big day. Rickey and I were about to go down in the water to be baptized at Lively Hope Baptist Church.

Chapter 4

Good Girls go to Catholic Church

During summer vacation one year, for some odd reason we went to Vacation Bible School at Holy Family, a Catholic Church. All I knew about a Catholic Church was what I had seen on TV, and so far there were no flying nuns at Holy Family, just solemnness. I did learn going in with all the statues; that they seemed to worship other people who hung out with Jesus, like St. Paul, Mother Mary, St. John, and so forth, but I wasn't familiar with any of that. Jesus was the only one I knew who died for me so I kind of just stuck with that.

I went along with following the ritual while I was there but going in a dark booth to talk to a man about my sins wasn't happening! Back then, folks told your mama and daddy. That belt you had already been acquainted with wasn't something you'd forgotten. So the Catholic thing was not working for me in the Baptist home, where you were taught spare the rod, spoil the child. I guess we were pretty good kids. I don't remember us getting the rod excessively. The Catholic Church also offered something else we were not accustomed, and that was white teachers and priests who took care of black kids. For the most part, we had only seen our mothers and grandmothers caring for white kids. There were no problems. We enjoyed the summer program, and of course, they offered great lunches, new friends from other schools, the newest playground equipment, and a lot of laughs as we tried to mimic the nuns and priests.

Chapter 5

Change On The Horizon

The time had arrived, and the tenacity of Mom had paid off. The money for the down payment for the new house is in pocket and the search is on. No more renting!! Not only tenacious, but mom was also astute when it came to finances, something she inherited from her dad.

My granddaddy was Mr. Alonzo Duncan, the Sou-Northern guy. That's my term for the southern men who moved north to get better jobs or whatever but always came back south cause they couldn't get enough of those southern girls. That term also encompasses South-Western and South- Eastern guys as well. (Don't Act like you don't know what's up.) Frankie Beverly and Maze even had to make a song about us, "Southern-Girls." My grandmother and he were never married. When I asked why she just said he was kind of mean and she said when he asked, she refused. Of course, I was the first-born grandchild to them both so I couldn't figure out what she meant by him being mean because all I ever saw from him and her was fun and love.

"Mother," as we called my grandmother Lillian, was a very easy going, quiet, and kind of shy person. At the time, with all the changes that were going on in our lives and that were

Janet Evans

about to take place, she was becoming more readily available. As a matter of fact, mom had completed her nursing courses and gave up her job as a nanny/housekeeper for the well to do over the mountain couple. Grandma Lillian "Mother" was offered the job, although she lived in Talladega, County, 50 miles away. She gladly accepted the offer because it was more money and allowed her more time with my brother and I through the week after she got off work. The people liked her so much they offered to buy her a house not very far from their home, but Mother refused the offer. That's why I said my mom got her business savvy from her dad, Mr. Alonzo Duncan. I guess I understood grandma was a small-town country girl and didn't want to live in the "big city."

Now it seems that everything turned out for the best. About the same time there was the incident where a psycho killed the only white man with authority that even had an ounce of justice or equality for our people. It's funny how some things even as a child are etched in your mind, the day the President of the United States John Fitzgerald Kennedy, was assassinated. It was the first day of my life that I had ever seen any of our people cry for the loss of any white man. I had learned at nine years of age that not all white people were haters of black people. Not all white people agreed with the mistreatment and disrespect of our people. Not all black people were pretending to care for whites or even like them. Maybe that was somewhat precocious for a nine-year-old but let me tell you, some children are serious about many things at an early age. So never take for granted that you're not teaching them life's lessons even without saying a word to them directly.

Chapter 6

New Houses Not Home

The perfect house was located in the perfect neighborhood where few whites remained right across the street from Pratt Elementary School. Only a few white children still attended but not for long. As we were moving in, they were moving out. It's so ironic that once again the Temptations had just come out with another song that seemed to epitomize what's going on in our lives, entitled Ball of Confusion, "People moving out, people moving in, why because of the color of their skin run, run, run but you sho' can't hide." Well, that was just fine because we had wonderful neighbors and friends. By this time, the house became that tangible reality and we for sure were partaking of the long awaited vision. The house was beautiful with all its perks; right across the street from the school, the #6 transit stopped right in front of our door. The other people moving into the neighborhood were people who had accomplished the dreams of someday owning their own homes as well. This was a great incentive for everyone to take exceptionally good care of what they had worked so hard to attain and a chance for their children to know that blacks can also have a part of the American dream. The Brady Bunch didn't have anything on us baby! After all, there were six of them and the 3 girls shared a room, and the 3 boys shared a room. Al-

Janet Evans

though the two of us, Rickey and I, had to share a room we had new twin beds. Our bedroom door was a stable style, where the bottom half and the top were separated making our room way cool. What more could we ask for, we had our own room. By this time, boys started liking girls and girls liked the Jackson 5. Every girl in the world, black an white, was hanging posters on their walls of Michael, who was our favorite because he was cute and our same age. We all had the biggest crushes on each of the four older brothers. Every girl I knew was going to marry one of the Jackson5. Once again about this same time the Temps came out with a song, "Just My Imagination." I think that was no coincidence either. Afros were wide and large and so were bell bottom pants and hot pants were HOT...HOT...HOT! What more could we ask for? We had our own home, bedroom, the Jackson 5 and Soul-Train. So, with all the white people moving out more of us moving in, it only inspired us to understand that together blacks had power. We were balling out of control back then. I don't care what rappers say, "Ball of Confusion" was the first rap song I ever heard way before Curtis Blow, Easy E, and MC Lyte. Now the ball was really about to get rolling.

Let me tell you, we were about to become a two car family. My mom's dad, the SouNorthern guy, worked for Buick right outside of the Motor City and was coming to Birmingham with a Buick Skylark for his daughter. No more catching the #6 downtown to over the Mountain. My dad joined an S&S Club named The Handsome Bruts. I remember how women were always commenting on how handsome he and my brother were. They would say "I know this is your boy; he's so handsome, the spitting image of you" so him joining the Handsome Brutes Club was a must.

I learned what a handsome brute was without Webster's dictionary. A good looking man who needed to stay single, one who felt that a woman should take care of the children alone and have his food cooked and hot on the table no matter what time he came home. If not, he'd give her trouble. Each Friday after work, especially a payday weekend, was an unwanted adventure to look forward to because the drama was on. The Saturday night wrestling match and not the one I enjoyed watching with my Grandma Lillian, no this one played out in our house. Several times the Saturday night matches ended with lamps and chandeliers broken as Rickey and I cringed from fear. The new house was no longer a home but a Ball of Confusion.

Chapter 7

The Shout

We looked forward to the weekend to visit "Mother," Grandma Lillian. She didn't live so far down in the country that there were no streets or street lights. She lived in a government housing project. At that time projects were not a place where drugs infested the community as it is today. Although I did experience seeing some people laid out on the lawn from the shout. Yes, I said the shout not shot.

The people were gathering in the evenings after work in the front yard of a lady's apartment. That wasn't unusual to see in Black neighborhoods especially mothers who have dinner cooking on the stove or in the oven, coming outside to keep an eye on us kids as we played in the big tree that was in the yard, or even to share the day's work experiences with each other. At home in Birmingham, I remember before we moved into the house when we lived in the apartments, the next door neighbor was sitting out with my mom and the neighbor on the other side of her one evening and her husband didn't like her outside with other ladies whether she was watching her children or not. When he came home, she became very nervous and uneasy to the point that once he pulled up and got out the car, she didn't know what his reaction might be. This day he screamed at her and beckoned for her to come here! When she got up from the chair she sat in was wet and so were her clothing. Although he was handsome, her husband wasn't a member of the "Handsome Brutes Club," but he should have joined. I learned early on what men can be like and later on how much women can change.

About twenty years later, I worked at a hospital where I was a phlebotomist. I was going into a patient's room to draw his blood on the burn unit. As I entered the room of this patient, I was shocked to see the husband of the nervous, frightened woman laid up bandaged from almost feet to head. Now these artists writing these songs back then must have been tracking our lives cause it seemed like his wife had to be listening to "A Thin Line Between Love and Hate" by the Persuaders. I asked Mr. Ray what happened to him and he answered, "Bertha did it to me. She went crazy and threw hot boiling water and grits on me."

Anyway, back to the shout. As the ladies at Grandma Lillian's apartments gather in the front yard to have church, I thought to myself, "That's different." They don't do this in Birmingham." Oh, but these women were what I was taught to be known as sanctified and as they would put it, filled with the Holy Ghost!! By now, I'm about 11 years old. My recollection of hearing about the Holy Ghost was that it was only for Pentecostal Sanctified people. As church service began, I watched from afar. Then when they really got crunk, I drew closer. They had music that allowed you to clap your hands and move. Hey, that was even encouraged! No "set still and be quiet." That was different. Then the people started to shout and dance. What was this? I decided to have a little talk with Jesus on this subject. In pure sincerity, I asked Jesus if this is real, let me feel it. As soon as I asked, the Holy Spirit fell on me, a power came over me and I was moving myself. DID I SAY GOD IS REAL? Those ladies prayed for me and I was saved to a new dimension. I didn't know I was no longer allowed to wear pants or shorts. Yet because Jesus had answered me by allowing me to experience His presence confirming to me it was real. I was fine with that. After all, I hadn't had an encounter that came close to this since age six.

Now going back home to Birmingham to the new house, school and die-hard Baptist household was quite interesting. I came back home only wanting to wear dresses and going to church with the only friend I knew whose family attended the shouting and praising kind of church. My parents didn't encourage me. They just let it run its course and by the time summer was over I had backslid. Nevertheless, I had come to know another dimension of Jesus—Holy Spirit.

Chapter 8

The ClothesLine

We moved into the new house. By now, Mom worked at the hospital nursing. Dad was no longer working out of town. He would get home before Mom at little after 5pm and we knew the rules.

1. No children in the house.
2. Food already prepared, eat, and clean the dishes.
3. Clean your room.
4. Do your homework.
5. If allowed to play outside on Friday before Dad gets home, do not leave the yard.
6. When the street lights come on be inside.
   Rules #5 and #6…BROKEN…

Never forget that your children are just that—children. If Rickey and I weren't playing together, it didn't matter. We knew how to buddy up to cover for one another to go play. So, we made rules of our own.

1. One of us had to be the watch out.
2. Make sure the phone volume is turned up high and close enough to the door to be heard.
3. Whoever answered had to say the other one was

Janet Evans

either outside talking to a friend or in the bathroom.
4. If we were able to play outside in the yard on Friday evening before Dad got home, we both had to be on the lookout as we played in someone else's yard down the street.

Price for breaking rules #5 and #6

It was getting time to go back home to our yard when the alarm went off. It was Dad's car coming up the main street. I said let's go Rickey we gotta to make it to our yard, the street lights are on and our yard is 5 houses away. Running with all breaks off we took off, dropping whatever we were holding at the time. Adrenaline was pumping. We were jumping off and over everything in our way, except for the cloth line.

Now, if you're going to have a clothesline, I would recommend that you leave a couple of pieces of clothing preferably, red or neon hanging on there at all times. Just for those idiot kids that may be running full force and not recognizing that invisible potential hanging post could cause serious bodily harm.

I was running so fast I ran straight into the neighbor's cloth line, not rope but wire. My adrenaline was so high I bounced right off the line and kept running once I regained my breath, beating Dad inside. I locked myself in the bathroom but by then the burning had intensified and looking at my neck in the mirror was even more horrifying than the burn itself. It was as if someone had tried to decapitate me. Oh, the waterworks were on and the screaming. Rickey came to the rescue first, what's wrong with you- but before he got the question out he saw my neck. Uhhhh!!!! How'd you do that? What you gon tell daddy? Man, you always messing up something!!! Just then Dad steps in, "What's wrong Jan?" "I was running and playing in the yard and ran into the clothesline." Dad lets the toilet lid seat down, sits and starts taking stuff out of the med-cabinet. Let me put something on that he said, "It's a pretty bad cut there."

I'm still looking scared for more reasons than one. Eyes bucked with tears still flowing and seemed like my neck was getting hotter; in anticipation of him realizing our clothesline was much too high for me to have had this near decapitation take place in our yard. I guess he was blinded by the drama I was displaying at the moment and feeling sorry for me. I watched him reach for that bright red liquid in the yellow bottle known as Mercurochrome. I was alright with that, then iodine, "OK" then Merthiolate, everyone knew Merthiolate burned more than Mercurochrome. "I don't want that one NO!! Then the cure- all Vaseline and then the most dreaded of all Alcohol, that's when I lost it, trying to run and getaway. It was too late he already had me locked in with those legs. He was merciful and only used Mercurochrome and Vaseline. He said we would wait for Mom to get home and take a look. That's when I really lost it. My mom was not going to let me off as easily as Dad. She was going to ask all the questions that I didn't want to answer. Rickey just stood in the doorway shaking his head.

Chapter 9

Used My First Bottle Of Alcohol

At age 11, my first bottle of choice was J&B Scotch. I used the whole bottle and never felt the least bit tipsy, but one boy in the neighborhood would get tore down. That green and red J&B bottle, I shall never forget my first hit.

It was a warm day at play and my friend who lived 3 doors away from me wanted me to play at her house. She said she wanted to show me something. I hurried over after the lunch my mom prepared and on a full stomach, I was ready to go visit Kimie. Turned out she wanted me to know about their next-door neighbors' wild parties that had been taking place in their backyard. The neighbors' backyard was surrounded with a bit of a privacy fence. When one of the boys came outside, we talked our way into the backyard to see what Kimie wanted to show me. He wasn't aware of what we were up to. Once we had gained entry, Kimie asked the boy about the parties his mom was throwing in the backyard. When we saw the empty cans and whiskey bottles lying around, I was not surprised because that was not unusual for people having a party.

The problem started when I picked up a bikini bottom with a stick and threw them saying they had no pool in the yard. The boy was angry with me and began to tell us to get out their yard.

He was being very aggressive, and he was very tall, all in my face screaming. I noticed my friend, Kimie, talking to someone behind me.

It was the other brother now both were angry that we had mentioned the parties and me swinging the bikini bottom around didn't help the situation. I was not about to be double-teamed by two brothers, one standing in front of me and the other behind me. I had to think fast. Like I said, earlier empty cans and bottles left from the parties were laying around in close proximity. Now Kimie was known for hitting and running, so she was probably going to throw a blow or two and take off running. My self-preservation instinct kicked in. My thought was to make use of the J&B bottle on the Pitbull bringing up the rear and the giraffe in the front might not want any. Either way, I was not letting go of that J&B whiskey bottle.

So as the younger brother that was built like a pitbull got more aggressive the fear formed into adrenaline and the left hand caused me to use J&B whiskey for the first time not as a drink but as a weapon. I crowned him Royal. Blood shot everywhere and the giraffe began to squeal like a stuck pig. My clothes were bloody and my converse sneakers. They both ran toward their house for help. Their mom was at work. I held onto the J&B bottle and headed home; Kimie made her usual escape. When I got to my house, I set the J&B Scotch bottle in the corner and went into the house. When Mom heard me, she came into my room and saw blood on my clothes and shoes. She asked what happened. Then I sang like a canary, eyes bucked telling her how I had just used the J&B Scotch bottle on the neighbor's boy because two of them were going to beat me up. Mom said she needed to go to see about the child.

Janet Evans

When she got there, the aunt had already gotten there to escort them to the emergency room. Later that evening, they returned not alone but with 28 stitches down the front of his face and their girl cousin who swore she'd take me down. So, for a while I kept the J&B whiskey bottle hid in the corner on the front porch. That's when I learned to never back a person in a corner because you never know how they'll come out of it or what they might come out with. I was still not a bad girl, just a scared one.

Chapter 10

Where Is Mama?
Remembering the first word of knowledge I received...

The pressing comb was hot on the kitchen stove and I was drawing up my shoulders as Mom was combing through my hair preparing the next section for the hot comb application. I was praying that hot hair pomade and hot comb didn't cause me to jump out the chair. I loved my hair looking good. The price of getting it to look like the girl on the Sunday school book cover was costly. I'm not speaking of the cost to a beautician. The threat of getting popped on the neck caused me to cower from the sound of the hot comb. Believe me, I was so glad when the afro came on the scene. What a great option and believe me I was signing up for one right away as soon as I got a little older. Mom was a stickler for keeping my hair groomed so it was a weekly ordeal.

This particular evening something strange was taking place at the same time. We heard the phone ringing in the den right next to the kitchen. The hair grooming process was interrupted as Mom went to answer the phone. I heard a voice speak to me softly and calmly "Something is wrong with Mama." That is what we called my Great Grandma Legulia who was my Grandma Lillian's mama.

After my mother returned to the room, she said rather nervously "Ok Jan I got to finish this hair. We got to go." Mama (Great-Grandma Legulia) is missing, and no one has seen her since noon. I knew something was wrong with her before Mom could get off the phone because of the "Word of Knowledge" that I had just received. To hear her confirm what I had just heard in my spirit was quite surreal. Mom was very nervous and upset and so was I, for more reasons than one. Yes, I was greatly concerned for the whereabouts of Great Grandmother Legulia but also about my mom getting back in my head with that hot comb, upset and rushing to finish my hair as we are about to rush from Birmingham down to Sylacauga, fifty miles away.

Thank God my Dad was there to drive us because at this point Mom really needed him to be a support to our family. I much later found out that my Dad had a sobering experience in a dream the night before that still to this day remains as vivid in his mind as it did the night he had it. He dreamed of a man that he could not see his face but knew him by his statue and complexion from the back. The man lived near GreatGrandma Legulia. He saw in the dream that the man hung a woman in a tree and cut her neck. The horror of the dream woke him. He got out of bed and couldn't sleep. In fact, he stayed up until he had to go to work that morning. By the time he returned from work that evening, we were on our way to find out what happened to Great grandma Legulia. He could not disclose to my mom the experience he had just hours before the phone call.

When we arrived at Great Grandma Legulia's, there were police, fire department, and rescue people along with flashlights and dogs. No one had found Great Grandma Legulia yet. Surely someone in the area has seen her, a cousin, an aunt, a neighbor, somebody. Hopefully, somebody will show up with her soon, right? Well, not that night, not the next day, week nor month or year, disappeared into thin air. What could have happened to a sweet little old lady that walked out to the mailbox and never returned? After months of searching that turned up no signs, the search parties ceased, and hope died with them.

Mom finally returned to work. Our food was always salty because of the tears that she shed daily as she prepared our meals. The only way to describe that period of time is numbness, but with numbness, there is at least hope of the return of the rush of stimulation that will bring the joy of restoration, but it never did. If we could at least find Great Grandma's body, it would be acceptable because now we must face it even without a body, she must be dead. How do you release a person when there is no body to release?

No more visits on summer break to the little house down in the country in the woods. No more feeling safe and secure. Not even in what was thought to be the safest place on earth. Great-grandmama Legulia's house far away from the Big City, "where too much goes on and you have to be careful over there," as they would say.

Finally, after a year something like eighteen months a man was out hunting miles away from where "Mama" Legulia lived when he stumbled upon what he thought at first was a dolls head. He got closer and discovered it to be the full skeletal remains of a female. Once he reported it to the police our family was contacted and she was identified based on old shoes and clothing. Finally, we were able to lay her to rest. Hopefully, one day this cold case file will be more than just another unsolved mystery because a loved one was taken without an explanation and gone without a goodbye.

Chapter 11

Joy Returns

The following summer promised to bring new expectations of joy and excitement, a new adventure for us as a family. We were about to travel to Flint, Michigan, to visit my Granddad, my mom's dad, who always brought joy and excitement to Rickey and I. Along with my uncles being four boys and my mom being the only girl and the oldest always made for lots of jokes, teasing, and oh yea gifts. Only this time we were going to visit them, not only them but all the family and places we had never been to.

Once we arrived, the long ride to get there seemed worth the thousands of times we asked our parents how much longer and "are we there yet." For sure we were restless once we'd eaten all the great snacks, sandwiches, and drinks mom packed in the picnic basket for the ride. We were ready to mingle although we were both rather shy. One thing for sure shy or not we couldn't wait to see my mom's brothers even though we knew they would tease us mercilessly. We loved it and wouldn't have it any other way.

They not only wanted us to visit Flint, but they said they were planning us a trip over to Canada, our first trip out of the

USA. WOW!!! Once there our travel landed us up in Toronto. That sparked a great desire in me to see the world. As we traveled thru the tunnel into another country, I felt as though the world must be explored; we are put here to see it, and I needed to see more.

Once back in Flint, we played with the kids next door on Baker Street. My imagination really sparked a desire to explore new things so I decided we would play being the newest superstars. I saw an old pallet in the backyard at Granddad's, so I said we need boxes to put around it for walls and draw windows and curtains for the backdrop. The creative artist was born over that summer and the new friends had to participate in playing on the stage.

The visit came to an end too soon. The summer vacation was over. It was time to say goodbye to our family and head back south. The long journey back home was never as exciting as the ride up but that time it was filled with the joy of much-fulfilled expectation. This had turned out to be a trip that inspired much dreaming for the future.

Chapter 12

Back to Life, Back to Reality

Time passed and another summer was upon us. The hot days brought out the hot pants, Baby! Nothing new under the sun, right, we just change the names. The hot pants were equivalent to today's daisy dukes and short shorts. Once again, I like adding new words to the dictionary. I think they should be called cheekys. The girl who lived up the street had long legs that made hers look even shorter, which was her business until she made it mine.

When I noticed, even though I was playing with my friends, that she waited until my Dad was outside washing his car (which was all the time) and my mom was at work or went to the store, to stroll down the street to hold a conversation with my Dad. Well, no, you don't!! I walked up and said, "What are you doing down here talking to my Dad when my mom is not here?" Dad said to me, "Don't be talking like that." I walked off and said, "She needs to get away from here, and I was telling my mom," as I went in the house sly way slamming the door. She was gone as quickly as I went in the back door and came back out. That was my Daddy, and no other women or girls had any right to my Daddy.

That whole ordeal made me realize exactly what my Mom was dealing with. These are the kinds of things that can cause weekend after weekends of fights. I was angry from the hostile environment my brother and I had to endure. Then I came to the conclusion that some men need to be single because it was just too hard to stay with them. I had seen enough and so had Rickey.

The next incident I remembered was one that had gone from bad to worst. The breaking of the chandeliers and lamps were getting closer together. The final turning point came when Rickey went to intervene in a fight with a hammer in his hand. Was he going to use it on our Dad? I'm pretty sure that was the so-called deal-breaker for Mom. The nefarious thought of what Rickey had on his mind that day must have frightened my Mom into ending the fight and the marriage. Seeing how the fighting was affecting us, we all learned a house doesn't make a home.

The fear of starting over, being alone, or not being able to financially survive was no longer enough to keep the marriage together. Sometimes it takes a greater fear of what would be to deliver us from what is. As Bob Marley sang, "fear was her only courage," so I learned fear has 2 strong forces working through it:

(1) to drive a person or (2) paralyze them. Fear will cause you to stay in a relationship that you should have walked away from or in some cases ran as fast as you could have from. Most of the time it's true a person will tell you who they are by their actions so it's best not to argue with them and believe them the first time. I wish I was paying more attention in this classroom of life because as you will find out later, I must have really suffered more injury than I originally thought from the cloth-line

Janet Evans

hanging experience. The cutting of my neck must have also cut off the air from my windpipe that gave oxygen to my brain, causing brain damage in this area of reasoning.

I am convinced that we will often be drawn to men like our dads whether or not we are conscious of it, even if we were not necessarily reared by them. My theory is this: that because of that wild gene and chromosome pool, you will innately be drawn to what's in your genetic make-up. Although you can't physically see any of these genes or chromosomes at work, in daily life and interactions, somehow, they are most definitely adhering to like genes and chromosomes in others, attracting these people to us. Laugh if you want. Then explain to me why my daughter and I are still trying to figure out how in the world, I mean the entire world, did she end up in a relationship with a guy like her dad, who did not raise her. I thought there was not even a remote chance that there was another person anywhere in this hemisphere that even came close to being the kind of person her dad was until she showed up with this clone at my door. Then as I thought more about it turns out my dad, her dad, and her baby's daddy all have some of the same strong characteristics. Will somebody please plead the Blood of JESUS!!

Chapter 13

Let's Do It Again

Now the tenacious Maggie (Mom) had gotten courage and a game plan together. Even though they had accomplished the goal of owning the dream house, they had not accomplished creating a safe, healthy environment for a home. Rather than living in the chaos of the house, she decided to live in peace by starting all over and finding a new home. By that time Rickey and I were no longer babies; we were old enough to understand what was about to take place. I'll never forget when Mom sat us down and said, "Jan and Rickey, I'm leaving your Daddy. This is not a good way to raise you all, with all this fighting and arguing. I've found a place to move; y'all won't have to change schools. It's your choice to live with me or your Dad. I'm not taking you from him. I think you are old enough to make up your own minds, whether you want to go with me or stay with your Dad. I'm leaving him in this house and starting over. I've already filed for divorce."

We both wondered what had taken her so long to make the decision. We both chose to move with Mom. Maggie was gone without a fight and without notice, gone for good. Rickey and I still loved our dad. We just didn't like him being married to our Mom. No more fear of someone being hurt or the anticipation of the next Friday night brawl. As a child you should be happy go lucky, not learning survival skills, but I have learned things such as you might as well expect men to cheat; don't trust them to take care of business for you; don't put up with being pushed around; if he fights, fight back and never come back; you might as well be a bad girl because good girls end up unappreciated and disrespected. Then after leaving a man, you find out if he really loves his children as a father or if he was trying to hold on to the woman. You understand that if he is truly a father (protector, provider, and nurturer), he will always remain just that throughout their lives, regardless of the relationship with their mother.

Chapter 14

Crushing of the Good Girl

Notice the good girl and the bad girl is the same girl, an undeveloped woman. What happens to many women is that their perception of what a husband and father are supposed to be becomes distorted during their developmental transition from a girl to womanhood. The self-preservation mechanism kicks in and in that immature state, we form a pseudo protective shield. We say no man is to be trusted and if not trusted not much respect follows. We say that I must expect failure from the man, to whom God has given authority to protect, provide, and nurture my life. When that wounded girl is crushed, the anger, rejection, and lack of nurturing turns her from sweet, sugar, and spice and everything nice to do unto them before they do it unto you.

The most crushing moment as a girl wasn't the divorce because we saw that coming and could actually see how that might be best for all involved. After all, we still were able to spend time with both Mom and Dad, we could still spend the night and weekends with dad and visit with our friends. So, what could be bad about that? It was a year or so of weekend visits to what once was our home and neighborhood. One particular Saturday due to a last-minute decision, I was dropped off at

Janet Evans

my girlfriend's just to spend a few hours there and my mom was picking me up. This was incidentally the same one who had been with me when I used the JB Scotch bottle. Interestingly she was usually somewhere around when trouble came my way.

This day she asked me a funny question after we had hung out for a couple of hours. She asked, "Aren't you gonna have to go get changed?" "Changed," I replied? "Yea so you can get ready to go?" "Go, go where," I asked? She replied, "Stop playing girl, ready to go to the wedding." I said, "What wedding? I don't know what you're talking about?" Then the most crushing words I had ever heard came from her mouth as she said, "You really don't know? You're not in the wedding?" She was as shocked as I was. She said, "What? Your Dad didn't invite you and Rickey or tell you he was getting married today?" What? My heart was so broken, and the embarrassment was just as bad. I had not gotten betrayed by a boyfriend yet, but my own Dad. I was totally taken back, totally devastated that all the other kids in the neighborhood knew about it except, my brother and me.

I immediately called my mom to come to pick me up. I cried all the way home as I explained to my brother the news. He was mostly controlled as he comforted me. How could my father not invite us or tell us? Who was this woman he was marrying and didn't even bother to introduce to us? After all, we're supposed to be part of the package, right? That was the proverbial straw that broke the camel's back. The wounded little girl harbored rejection and anger which made for a bad girl. As Proverbs 18:14 says "The human spirit can endure a sick body, but who can bear a crushed spirit." (NIV) Another lesson confirming what I already believed, trust no man with your heart— they are cheaters. It's best to play the game after all my older cousins would tell me all the time "you're gonna break some hearts slim with those long legs and big eyes. So now I'm seeing it's better them than me, that's for sure. Love was a game for fools. So, the good girl is gathering hunter's arrows (valuable information for further use). I needed to know how the hunters got captured by the game.

Chapter 15

The Father's Heart

The situation soon turned for the better. I am convinced that God the Father will use kind-hearted people to love us and show us His heart. That's why Proverbs 68:5 says, "He is a father to the fatherless and a defender of widows is God in his holy dwelling."

Now my Mom was dating this man I'll never forget and always appreciate, Mr. George Jackson Jr. He had no daughter and only one son. He took to my brother and me as close as any dad would. He showed the concern for us we needed. He made sure we knew his family, took us to visit with him, and gave me a surprise 16th birthday party in Montgomery at his mom's house where all his nieces and nephews came to celebrate with us. He took us to Atlanta to the Underground. No Christmas passed even after he and my mother split that he didn't reach out to bless us. He was always respectful and available, even to the next generation. He bought my kids go-cars for Christmas; the love is genuine even to this day. I love to call him and spend time with him although he does most of the grilling which he is well known for. I try to find as many ways as I can to show him how much we appreciate his love and kindness throughout the years. Even though he didn't talk to me about God, my God Father showed me the Father by putting our needs before his own. Giving us what was not his obligation to give, while showing God's unmerited favor to us. He even bought me cars over the years. Remember this ladies, no man can buy you if you're not for sale. Genuine love comes from the heart and will give and do for you from that place. May I add, without any dangling of the carrot before you and without any demands attached.

Chapter 16

Tiger Country

Now I was about to transition to be a young lady and, more importantly, a Fairfield High School Tiger. The tenacious Maggie had decided that it was time to move on to another side of town and purchase us another home. I think moving to another area was good for us all. Since we had still been attending school right across the street from Dad's house until then. Rickey and I found it would have been a little awkward to take it upon ourselves to just drop in after school. After not being introduced to his new wife, she now occupied the house that was once home to us. My mom, as usual determined Jan & Rickey will have a home and Fairfield is just as good a town as any. She purchased us another house and the timing was great. We had just enough time for us to make friends a couple of years before going into high school. The change of environment didn't take much adjustment. The new school, neighborhood, and friends to add to the old ones we already had were a bonus. Most of all seeing our Mom happy and achieving her goals was what we wanted. Not only did Mom purchase one home for us to live in, but later, she got another one down the street as a rental property. She exceeded her dream of one day being a homeowner.

Chapter 17

Davee and Helen (Big Helen)

Our long-time family friends that Mom knew when she first moved to Birmingham about 12 years earlier also lived near us. They became more like God Parents. To seal the deal, they had two sons. Their younger son had an absolutely gorgeous baby boy and ironically, his name was the same as my brother Rickey. They also had one daughter who was hydrocephalus and oh how they loved and cared for her. My job was to care for Lil Rickey, as we called him, and I was excited to do just that. Also, at 15 years old with a driver's permit all I needed was a licensed driver and my Godmother Big Helen was my ticket. She always wanted help with the baby and driving her to the store or visit her friend some Friday evenings. This was her routine. She could count me in as long as the Fairfield Tigers weren't playing a home game.

Some other times I chauffeured her to her friend's house while her husband gave her a break from caring for Evonne, who we called "Pumpkin Pie," their special needs daughter. I could see how my Godfather, Davee, loved, and cared so much for his wife and kids. It was a blessing for me in more ways than one to be around them. It allowed me to see another man other than Mr. George Jackson that loved and cared for someone other than themselves and would go the extra mile to convey that love in deeds.

Davee did everything for his daughter as much as his wife: bathed, clothed, fed, took her out for exercise until she was unable, even then he'd push her on the front porch in her wheelchair to let her catch a fresh breeze or the sun. How he loved her, patting her on the hand, kissing her on her enlarged head, pinching her cheeks, making her smile, and she would flash the most beautiful dimples as she laughed out loud. How I admired him for that. The love and patience Davee showed for his family was a blessing to see. Helen, affectionately known as Big Helen, would say Big Jan come and take me over to the Davis's house.

Everyone knows a teenager with a permit will drive you to the moon. Many Friday evenings Big Helen, Big Jan, and Lil Rickey headed across town to the Davis' to visit. Davee wanted his wife to have an outlet from caring for Pumpkin Pie all week, although he had worked all week himself at US Steel. I saw then that some good men still existed. He was also a deacon at the church we now attended. Not only did I see how he interacted at home but also at church. He showed me a faithful man.

The new life was going just fine, even if my freshman year as a Fairfield Tiger had started off with a boycott. The school had been predominantly white until 1969, and after four years of integration there had been no black cheerleaders or homecoming queens. They only had black athletes and the senior class of 73 refused to graduate and leave behind that legacy of injustice. The boycott was on and crossing the picket line was not going to change things for the new freshman class. I stood with the upperclassmen to resist the injustice of oppression and discrimi-

Bad Girl Virtuous Woman

nation. What a way to start your freshman year of high school. Yet after the boycott was over and successful, it opened the door for me to become elected sophomore Queen and an alternate for my junior year, which suggests some degree of popularity amongst my peers. Things were going pretty well for the family.

My brother and I were latch key kids because Mom was now working the 3p.m. -11p.m. shift so through the week we were out of school at 3p.m. while mom was at her job. Hanging out at Big Helen and Davee was a perfect situation for me. Big Helen and Davee's oldest son's girlfriend and her friends from Miles College hung out with us at Big Helen's sometimes as well. These young women often talked about life and would give me some good advice. Things like stay in school, don't be-lieve guys, they are all after one thing, don't be in a hurry to give them what they want, because it's not all that great the first time anyway. Wait until you're grown and you don't want a baby; it will ruin your future. I did feel a lot more mature hanging out with them. They were, after all, college women. I figured they really did know what they were talking about. They all seemed to agree on the subjects discussed and had not long ago walked in my shoes; I took their advice to heart.

I had a football player who had a huge crush on me, who asked to take me annually to the football banquets. I attended all the way through my senior year. As other guys tried to talk to me, it was never anything serious going on. I was not getting intimate with any of them. I kind of figured out some were just trying to prove as we said in the 70s, that their rap was stronger. I let them try and by senior year no one had prevailed. They just couldn't figure me out. What they didn't know was that I had already decided on the guy I wanted, and he had already gradu-ated the year before. He was older, cooler, and one of the most

Janet Evans

handsome guys that had been at our school. Of course, he had a car. I was never a follower. I made my decisions and danced to the beat of my own drum.

Chapter 18

Making of a Bad Girl

Although the bad girl was being stirred up during the high school years, I can't say that anyone was responsible for my going down that road. I was just going to do things my way. Trying weed with my brother at 16 wasn't my idea, but since he gave me the joint while he smoked it and didn't go crazy. I tried it and liked it. Even though my weed smoking increased, I still attended church and sang with the choir on the weekend. At age 17, the year before graduation an unexpected incident occurred. The devil is always a likely aggressor. This was a day that Mom was at work and Rickey wasn't home either. I heard the doorbell and to my surprise, standing at the door, was the Pastor.

Umm, what does he want? I said, "Hey Pastor come on in. My mom's not here. She's at work." I think he knew that because her car was not in the driveway. But maybe he had something he wanted me to relay to her. He moved over to a chair and took a seat. I'm asking, "Ok, well Pastor is there something you want me to pass on to my Mom?" He said, "No, no not at all. I just wanted to talk to you. I see you'll be graduating before long and I was wondering what school you're planning to attend and what course of study are you taking? "I thought maybe the church is planning some type of scholarship money or special acknowledgment for us so he's here to gather information. Then he said, "Well you know Sis Laura's finished her nursing classes and passed her test. She's about to work as a RN you know." I replied, "Yes, I know." I honestly hadn't given much thought to it though. Why was he bringing this up? "Well," he said, "I know your Mom works hard and college is expensive and you'll need a car to get around. Lara needed help and I helped her get a car. Now are you taking birth control?" Now I'm feeling very uncomfortable discussing various forms of contraceptives with my Pastor especially in the private setting. Not only that I'm still a virgin and he was looking at me like the wolf that he was and I'm the lunch and Red Riding Hood.

Suddenly the doorbell rings, the door opens simultaneously, and in walks my Godfather, Davee, who is also a deacon of our church. Asking the Pastor as he is entering, "What are you doing here? Her mother is at work." Davee said, "You need to come on out of here. If you want to talk with her mom you need to call her ahead of time to arrange a meeting, so she can hear what you have to say." Needless to say, I never got any more popup visits from the Rite Rev.

Going to church and facing him on Sunday felt totally awkward. Now I was angry because now I didn't feel comfortable at my own church, where I have friends and it also put my Godfather in a sensitive position, although he never asked me anything concerning that day. I tried continuing to attend church there. It just wasn't the same. I wasn't interested in what the Rite Rev. had to say anymore. I felt uncomfortable and also ashamed for some reason each time I passed him in the corridor. Then I became angry. I felt it was best for me to leave, but why should I go? I didn't do anything. I can't sing in the choir anymore. Why do I have to lose out because of the Rite Rev's lack of character?

I never seduced him or enticed him to confront me in the manner that he did. So, God, why didn't you stop him? The way he looked at me now was hard to figure out what was on his mind, but I felt intimidated. I can't help but feel my friends saw the difference in my attitude toward the Pastor. I just couldn't deal with this. Eventually, I stopped attending church. One day the Holy Spirit said to me, "Why are you angry? I haven't done anything to you. A Pastor is just a man. Didn't I say not to put your trust in man." "Yes," I replied, "So why didn't you stop him?" Not sure how long it was before I realized it, but one day it came to me that God did stop the Rite Rev by sending Davee by my Mom's house at that very moment to intervene in the devil's plan of attack. That's what David's do; they kill off giants, bears, and lions to keep you from becoming prey.

Chapter 19

Change, Change, and More Change

After several years we had settled into the other side of town and adjusted to the new relationships. There were still some things that remained unchanged and one thing was Grandma Lillian, "Mother." She still came to visit from time to time and the love she showed us always let us know we were not rejected. She no longer worked for the over the Mountain socialites family in Birmingham. That family had also ended in divorce. "Mother"(Grandma Lillian) was working back in Talladega County. Still, anytime she could she came to visit, the time with her always brought joy. Watching wrestling matches with her on Saturdays as she shouted let him go!!! Put the sleepy hold on him! Then getting her crossword puzzle out of the newspaper to increase her knowledge because she only completed sixth grade. She would prepare to exercise her prowess in the kitchen, cooking the best tea cakes and fried apple pies you ever had anywhere. Her visits helped to anchor the house as a home even if it was just for the weekend.

After her visit it would be time to go back to check on Big Helen, Lil Rickey, and Pumpkin Pie. Big Helen would be joyful as usual when I showed up because she knew that when I showed up, she was about to get a break. I had a friend that loved babies as much as I did, and Lil' Rickey and I would head to visit her. We would play with him until he was completely worn out and by the time I returned him to Big Helen, all I had to do was bathe him and he was ready for bed. One day before we left Big Helen had cooked and was insisting that I eat some type of beans and something else that I really didn't want. Still a teenager, I'm thinking no thanks, burgers and fries are where we're headed. Big Helen said, "Big Jan you better eat cause I ain't cooking nothing else, and I told Davee I want these floors cleaned tonight before these folks come here." "Ok, I'll get some later," I said as I took Lil Rickey and rushed off to meet my friend. We need to get back before dark and I can get Rickey situated before going home myself. So, I finished and rushed off without eating any of the meal Big Helen had cooked.

The truth is many times changes happen much too unexpectedly and quickly. It was late somewhere between 12:30 and 1:30 am when Davee called and told my mom that he went into the room to check on Big Helen and she was gone. Really, she had died in her sleep. I was devastated, shocked in disbelief. In just a few days everything had changed. I could still see Lil Rickey and help out, but now Davee had to take care of both Lil' Rickey and Pumpkin-Pie. The oldest son lived only a few houses away and now stepped in to help out. Lil Rickey was about to reunite more with his natural parents. It was time for my life to move forward, just as time does. With Big Helen gone Davee needed help and their oldest son had a girlfriend who could help out and Davee needed room for a possible new wife. I needed to move on and take what I had experienced with me.

Chapter 20

Eye's Grown Now

Age 18 was coming up soon and like I said earlier, I was not a follower. I was just going to do it my way. Thank God for the advice of Big Helen and (Davee's oldest son's girlfriend) and her friends from Miles College who told me not to rush into sexual relationships. Well, they gave me the best advice they knew. I don't remember any of them saying just wait til' you marry. The thing is, I decided that I was going to wait until I was eighteen. The decision was going to be mine. Although I had talked to different guys and had them try. I was not letting some boy who was trying to experiment with sex make me his guinea pig. While the guys were trying to see who would bring the "strongest rap" and be able to conquer. I had already decided it would be the older guy, the coolest and most handsome guy with a car. When I chose my guy, it was what I had set in motion. I calculated even the very month. I was not even looking for love. I was emotionally detached, that was probably because I felt that guys really weren't to be trusted with my heart and that they all cheat. The college girls were also right about your first time having sex. That first encounter was something less than spectacular and I could have waited even longer.

The emotional detachment allowed me to not get my feelings

involved, so when he messed up, I had no problem kissing and saying goodbye. The other good advice I had gathered from my college friends was that "guys are like buses." There will always be another one coming along without you having to wait long at all.

    Then Mason showed up. He was sweet, and I liked him before I knew he was digging me. He was every bit as handsome and kept a job laying bricks until he joined the Navy. Before we got going good, my first shows up just to say hello unexpected and uninvited. When Mason saw him leaving, he was a little upset. He began questioning me and grabbing my arm, snatching me. I turned and like Catwoman, I left him with nail print memories of how not to do that again. He left and came back saying he was only trying to get me to stop walking away. We reconciled that drama, and actually he loved that I defended myself if needed. We really had a good relationship for a while. He left for the U.S. Navy, yet his letters and gifts continued. I liked him a lot.

Chapter 21

The Real World

Now it's time for embarking upon adulthood responsibility. So, I thought I wanted to exchange my Candy Striper uniform (extracurricular volunteer hospital work) for a real nurse's uniform.

At the same time God blessed me with my first full time job, straight out of High School working as a Phlebotomist/EKG Technician at BMC Princeton. They gave me on the job training. It was a great opportunity. I worked, went to college and partied. My attention span for school grew short. I had this one Harvard grad female instructor who made it practically impossible for me to keep up. Not only that my main focus was on saving enough money from my job to rent an apartment with new furniture. I was able to accomplish that goal and moved out of my Mom's house. The second year I was able to purchase a Pontiac Grand Prix and transferred to another hospital doing the same work. I ran into unforeseen issues with a couple of co-workers. For some reason, a couple of girls felt as if I was supposed to do all the extra tests. These tests required more time due to the collection process of carrying a machine into the room, finding a plug to keep the collection at a certain temp at 5am in the morning when the patients were most sound asleep. One morning I confronted one of the ladies about how the work was being distributed. She took the lab request I had off my tray and threw the one she had to me. As they went flying across the floor, "What would JESUS do?" was not the thing that entered my mind. I must confess that what I did was wrong. I do not encourage anyone to take this course of action. I told the coworker that I was tired of her and the other lady taking advantage of me. Even though I had just purchased that car and needed money to pay my bills, that was not a good enough reason to keep me from slapping her. Then I commenced to give her a good old Birmingham had enough whipping. After that I guaranteed she'd think twice before she ever treated or disrespected another black person the way she had done me. There were no excuses for my actions, but like I confessed earlier, I was more of a follower of Malcolm than our beloved Martin during that time. The Supervisor came in after hearing the commotion to let me know that she was not tolerating such behavior. I immediately informed her that I quit. She was not going to be given the privilege of firing me. I left that day without a job not knowing how I would be able to pay my bills. Yet I realized that I was a person who would risk all for the principles of what I believed and stood for even if I had to stand alone. So now what do I do? Talk to the Lord and pray for another door to open quickly. God, being the God of mercies, did just that within a month's time. I moved from B'ham to Flint, Michigan to work at a Methadone Clinic. I made more money and had many perks, one being nepotism which didn't allow anyone to deal unfairly with the bosses' niece based on the color of my skin. What a great setup my uncle being the Director of the Methadone Program. When that door opened so quickly for me, I felt as though God understood my position and had forgiven me for assaulting the coworker.

Janet Evans

Even after moving north, I ran into a woman who wanted to deal unfairly with me, maybe because I was new, young, and black. I really didn't know what her problem was. It really didn't matter because she shut down completely once she realized I was the bosses' niece. God turned it around for my good once again.

Chapter 22

The Call I Didn't Hear Coming

After only about four months of being in Michigan, I get a call that "Mother" (Grandma Lillian) is in the hospital and had a major stroke. I returned to Birmingham right away to see "Mother," the only grandmother I had, the one that loved and favored me as long as I could remember. She was my cheerleader, always hoping the best for me. As soon as I arrived I could see that "Mother" was in serious trouble. Her face was strained, her speech slurred and slow. She was happy when I got there. I stayed by her side and the most significant thing I remembered was that I sat by her bed that night and read her favorite scripture to her over and over; Psalms 23. The next few days things turned for the worst and then "Mother," Grandma Lillian was gone too.

Chapter 23

Entering the Lion's Den

Ironically during the same time one of my closest friends lost her granddad so we were hanging out together, comforting one another. Her sister and uncle came home from Cleveland. I had briefly met them when we were in high school. One day after both funerals were over and we were all getting ready to return North. The uncle offered to take us out with him and one of his friends who came down from Cleveland and also had family in B'ham. They took us out in his Baby Rolls Royce with all the bells and whistles. Along with weed, cognac, and cocaine. At age 20, life is about to take on a whole new dimension.

I have learned that when losing a close loved one, the enemy seemed to always show up in my life at a time when I'm most vulnerable. For Carly and I the experience was exciting. Older guys, 30ish with all the flash and lures. Rod, being Carly's uncle, we felt safe in their company. So, we both decided to snort the line as it was called. (The effect was nothing that caused a wild, hyper reaction.) Maybe it was because of the weeds calming effect that we were indulging in daily that just left me with an underwhelming experience.

I realize now that sometimes the loss of someone leaves a

void and our nature as human beings is to try to fill the void, whether it be with another person, place, thing, or all three. I call this writing yourself a "Nounscript" Let me explain, a noun is defined as a person, place, or thing. When there is a void in our lives, we tend to try filling those empty places. Usually by filling that void with another person, place, or thing in order to dull the pain of the loss. You do this by dulling the pain with a subsequent pain reliever or "prescription" known as a "Script." Therefore we are writing a "Nounscript." Losing "Mother" Grandma Lillian was hard and no one could ever fill her place. Although I tried self-medicating by "writing a Nounscript." Try not to do this, the void is real and not allowing time to heal your grieve really prolongs the process -many times, adding additional problems.

I had to get back to work in Flint. Carly's sister and uncle Rod had to return to Cleveland. As we discussed our itinerary, they suggested I travel as far as Ohio with them and save money by catching a flight to Flint from there. They would appreciate the help driving and the company. The travel date and time were confirmed, and with bags packed I headed back to my job. On the way back we were all having a great time. The foolishness we can exhibit in the name of "A Good Time" Let me stay right here for a moment because someone needs to understand that foolishness is defined as lack of good sense or judgment, stupidity, folly, idiocy, silliness, lack of foresight, imprudence, indiscretion, irresponsibility, rashness, and recklessness. Proverbs 15:5 tells us that we are born with an innate foolishness, but discipline will help train us in wisdom. The only problem here is that when you are the kind of person who's just gonna do it your way, discipline is not what you lend yourself to, but foolishness. The truth is many are lending themselves to foolishness these days even at the age they should be mature naturally and spiritually. A fool uses reasoning skills to make wrong decisions, so age is not a factor. Proverbs 19: 3 says, "A person's own folly leads to their ruin." The only saving grace I had was that of (Proverbs 14:1) did not apply to me, which states, "The fool has said in his heart there is no GOD." So you can behave foolishly without being a fool. I also recognize that we sometimes judge other's foolishness and somehow fail to notice our own. Simply by forfeiting to make our decisions based on wisdom. What is wisdom? The man known as the wisest man in the world, King Solomon, states in Proverbs 9:10 that the fear of the LORD is the beginning of wisdom. The word fear here actually refers to reverential respect. Which suggests that you deem GOD and his Word of the highest authority; and your reasoning skills that oppose His word as foolishness. Ok let's move on from this back to "having a good time" on the way back from Alabama to Flint by way of Cleveland. Still with a broken heart.

Chapter 24

Gabriel, Lucifer, or Satan

I'm told we are all given at least two guardian angels at birth. I also understand that Lucifer was Satan's name before he got a foot in his back and cast out of heaven. Lucifer means "bright star." Second Corinthians 11:14 tells us that Satan disguises himself as an angel of light.

The "NounScript" is about to be filled. Person: Rod, Place: Cleveland and Thing: "The Life" as it is referred to: extravagant parting, Dom Perignon, Remy Martin, high-end cars, penthouses, diamonds, travel, and drugs." At least that was as much of the definition that I had grasped. Once we made it to Cleveland, the flight to Flint was delayed another day in order for me to see Cleveland. It didn't matter that it was Sunday, or I would miss work Monday. The opportunity to party in Cleveland was there. Rod had taken the initiative to get me a flight set for Tuesday morning so I could still make it to work from the airport. They dropped me off at my hotel after making sure I was settled in comfortably. Rod then said, "I'm leaving this briefcase here with you." It was where he kept the drugs. Until then I had no idea how much was in the briefcase, only that it was in there. Once he opened it my thought was that he really wants to know if he can trust me. They left and I was about to get comfortable, take a shower and relax until time to go check out the after-hour club, "Winstons," that I had heard about anytime someone mentioned Cleveland. Since I had been left with this briefcase it dawned on me that Rod was not just having fun but was taking more interest than I originally thought. Before I got a shower, I realized I didn't have a cola to mix with my cognac, so I had noticed that the soda machine sat right next to my door when I came in. I grabbed change and stepped to the machine.

Unfortunately, the machine was out of order. Since it sat right at the stairwell, I assumed they probably had them positioned the same on each floor. I would just run up one flight and the soda machine would be right at the door. I didn't bother to go back in the room and get my key. I just ran up the stairs to the next floor. Much to my surprise when I entered my room, there stood a fully uniformed police officer. He was on the phone with the front desk, asking them who the room belonged to. As I entered the room the officer turned to me and asked, "Are you Janet Evans?" There was no need to deny it. My purse and ID were lying right next to the phone along with the briefcase full of weed and cocaine, and not a small amount either. The thoughts that ran through my mind at that moment were, "You'll be thirty-five years old before you get out of prison. I replied, "Yes, Sir." He hung the phone up and walked toward me as he glanced down at the briefcase where the drugs were on the bed. Then what he said next shocked me, "Ma'am, we've had some break ins over the last week. So, I would make sure to keep my door locked at all times." I said, "Yes, Sir, I will. The pop machine was broken so I just ran to the next floor and came right back. But I won't be doing that again." He then politely walked out and said, "Alright you have a great evening." No way this cop didn't see this setup spread out in this room. Was I scared? Yes!!!! I could have peed my pants, but if he was going to arrest me, there was no reason not to do it then. After All I could have flushed everything down the bowl if he was leaving to call for backup. I was just a young hundred thirty-pound female. He was 6'3" 280 lbs and didn't need any help handling me. What had just happened here? All I know to this day is that God is Good and Merciful. I for sho needed this drink and everything in this briefcase.

After getting a shower and laying down for a relaxing nap there was the strangest occurrence that took place. As real as you are reading the pages of this book. "Mother," Grandmother Lillian walked up to the bed and said, "Get Out Of Here." I said, "No, Mother, I'm alright," and then I sat straight up in the bed. I was still going to do it my way. Although the visitation still lingered in my mind, I had never had an occurrence of seeing someone who had passed on and so vividly. I was not to forget it.

The night comes and I'm about to get the tour of the city, which lasts till daybreak. We go get breakfast. After breakfast, I go back to the hotel to rest until time to be picked up again for the evening. The time spent with my new friends was so enjoyable. I didn't want to leave, but I needed to catch an early morning flight and get back to work.

By now the guy in the Navy and I had gotten kinda serious. He talked of me marrying him and his gifts were weighing on my heart. What he didn't know was that trust issues were still blocking my heart. He was probably not to be trusted that far away in Italy. He was a very good looking man so the ladies were surely at him and we were really too young for marriage anyway. Rod was thirty-six, had already been in the military Special Forces and earned medals, badges and was Green Beret.

Janet Evans

He was now established in his convenience store businesses and at least he's in the States. Right? I felt I needed a more mature man, the age difference between Rod and me didn't matter at all. Hey, my Dad's wife was only eight years older than me. Now I was just understanding that perhaps that's why my brother and I were not invited to my Dad's wedding, we were too old. Still feeling grieved about the loss of my Grandmother, I was ready to accept the love and attention from someone nearby and as doting as she was. It seemed like I'd just found that in Rod. With Rod grieving the loss of his Dad, he was feeling the same void. Maybe he was writing his own *Nounscript.

Chapter 24

Continues

During the week Rod called expressing how much he enjoyed our time together and would love for me to come back to visit one weekend when I was free. He said he knew I was still mourning the loss of my grandmother, but he hoped I would feel up to it soon. The next week he called to check on me and asked if coming back to Cleveland for the weekend was something that I might be interested in; I declined the offer. I just needed to rest and get back into the swing of things in Flint. He said he understood but wanted me to know it was a standing invitation. We talked on the phone often after that for weeks. Finally, Rod asked if he could drive over and spend the weekend in Flint so we could go out and spend some time together. Well, yes, that sounded like a better idea. At least I was on my own turf so to speak. If he was serious about wanting a relationship, he'd have to show me more. He showed up the weekend and we went out and enjoyed Flint and had a great time. When it was time for him to leave, he let me know he wanted to spend more time with me and had developed serious feelings for me. We were now about to define our relationship (always important ladies), never assume anything, ask questions. The following week he called and said, "I've already paid for your flight. This is your flight information, so

Janet Evans

when you leave work get to the airport and I'll be waiting for you when you land." OK! A man with a plan, I really liked that. Then every weekend after that for months his game plan was the same. When I arrived he would have piles of size 7/8 clothing he bought for me waiting. Then it progressed to jewelry. He said, "You know if you come to Cleveland you can work in one of the store. I will pay you what you're making on that job." I was not at all expecting that offer. I could see he had serious thoughts on where he wanted the relationship to go. I said I would really think about it. On my next visit, we visited his friend, Don, who lived in a nice apartment with a security entrance. Once we entered the apartment, I saw a picture of Natalie Cole and found out the guy was dating her. Once we left the visit Rod asked if I liked his friend's apartment. I said sure it was nice and he said the guy is moving out and that I could have it if I liked it. So, hey just like that I decided to move to Cleveland. After I got there he bought me a new contemporary living room set. He didn't even take me to pick it out. I was really impressed; I would have picked what he bought myself. I even loved the lamps. As for my job at the store, I went in to work one day and the next day I got ready and we ended up picking up his eight-year-old son and going to Aurora to Sea World. I never worked in the store again. I anticipated working and paying my own bills, then he said he knew I would work, but he had prepared to handle everything when he asked me to come to Cleveland.

He was like a guardian angel. He was the kinda man any woman would hope for. He was a handsome Man's Man. He was reliable, concerned, gentle, protective, well-off, and doting. He said all the right things. Even on my worst days when "the lady in red" showed up and I was cramping so bad, I couldn't get out of bed. He took such great care of me. One day I was curled up on the sofa polishing my nails, he looked at me and said, "I even love sitting here just watching you paint your nails." I knew then the hunter had got captured by the game.

    For you girls who really don't have a clue what I mean, let me enlighten you to knowledge of what you're really working with. For many of you have been deceived into thinking another woman is your competition. No Honey, that's not how this game is played. The man's natural instinct is to be a hunter, a conqueror, a victor. If he says he's not competitive, he is lying or a complete Loser. If a man is really into you, he will initiate the hunt, bend the bow and release the arrow. All of these call for a plan of thought, effort, knowledge and precision in order to hit the target. If you know anything about game sports, hunting, fishing, etc. You know it's the chase that's exciting. Once the game is captured the hunter experiences a certain euphoria so much so they will even want to take the game home not to consume but to hang on the wall and display his success. The problem for the hunter is that sometimes there are unassuming games. Some are cute, and furry, resembling household pets, while others appear to be deceptively slow and calm or just blend into their surroundings as if they are altogether not paying attention. While the hunter has initiated the hunt, bent the bow and released the arrow, the unassuming game has already positioned itself to gain the advantage on the hunter. For example, the cougar, also known as a mountain lion, puma, or panther is known to stalk hunters, usually just to observe their behavior and just fade away before the hunter can take notice. But on occasion, when a cougar attacks a hunter, he usually has no hint of the cat's presence until it's on top of him. The primary danger from a cougar is not being charged while hunting but being stalked and attacked before the hunter has time to get the gun to his shoulder. What am I saying? Know for what purpose

Janet Evans

you are being hunted, whether it's for consumption which will later be expelled or to be taken home, kept, and displayed as his greatest prize. Then unassumingly position yourself.

Then Rod began to tell me things about life and especially drugs and men. The things he said I valued as law because of the way he treated me. Always remember this he told me "Never take any wooden nickels," which means don't allow yourself to be cheated or duped; don't be naive. If a man can't treat you the way I do then don't listen to what he says but what he does. Other lessons included don't snort powder with people you don't know and NEVER smoke it because it could take you places I would never return from. He said value yourself. Even if a man doesn't see the value in you, you know you are a Queen and carry yourself in that manner. Walk away and don't look back if a man doesn't respect you. In this life which he often referred to, he told me to trust no one other than him because it's full of snakes. No one here knows anything about you, so keep it that way. The less they know about your business, the better. Of course, I kept all these things close to my heart.

Everything was great. When I wanted to visit Birmingham to see my family and friends for a week, he was good with that. Then by the fourth day he'd say, "Aren't you ready to come home. I miss you. So I would fly back earlier than planned. His niece Carly that introduced us still lived only about four blocks from my Mom, so during my time at home we were planning for her to come visit me when I got back. Carly's sister Rena lived in LA. Because I had never been to LA and wanted to go Rod flew me out to visit her and his sister Shelly, who lived in Hollywood on Mt Olympus. His sister Shelley and her husband owned machinery and contracted for Orange County; Shelley also owned a salon in Englewood. Their home was gorgeous, set among the celebrities. Shelley's home was decorated with pictures of her and her husband at events with Muhammad Ali, Don King, and others. I felt like I was living a dream. Seeing some of the celebs in the neighborhood was exciting. I was blinded by the glitz and glamour of "The life". Then it was time to go back to Cleveland to the man supplying the dream. It was time for another trip to his son's favorite spot SeaWorld to get soaked by the much loved Shamu, the Whale. He loved and adored his little boy.

The friend Kerry, who was in Birmingham visiting who drove the Roll Royce during the time of Rod's dad's death lived in Cleveland and was owner of an Insurance Agency, had two wives. Yes, and he and his two wives lived together. Now I had to ask Rod some questions once we left visiting their home. He needed to assure me he wasn't thinking along those lines. Not that they weren't nice people, but their religious beliefs permitted a polygamous lifestyle. That absolutely confirmed my belief that Islam was not for me. On a visit to another of his friends' homes, there were several young adults living there. A young woman engaged me in conversation most of the visit, while Rod and his friend sat in the kitchen talking. The visit lasted less than an hour, but the young lady was very hospitable offering me refreshments and movies. I thought she was just being friendly. After leaving Rod said she asked him if I was taken? What!!! Really, I realized I was a fish out of water. I had no idea the chick was gay or interested in me the whole time. I know people are people everywhere you go but these Ohio Players were really smooth.

Leaving Flint seemed to have been the right choice. I'd been in Cleveland about a year now and this man treats me like an absolute Queen. By now no one can convince me Rod was not

Janet Evans

my Guardian Angel. Not only did he treat me well, but he also went about doing good for families and children in and around the city. Bringing groceries and electric heaters to those in need, and paying their electric and gas bills. When parents had spent all their money on drugs, he gave school supplies, shoes, clothes, and even rat traps to people living in housing areas where the rats were literally the size of cats. At this point I'd realized that the stores were not the only business ventures Rod was involved in. He had decided to show me his philanthropist nature. Which I realized the reason he was coming out to help these people was because he had people who supplied drugs to and worked the whole area. He said these people were already on drugs and he was watching out for their families, because they weren't going to stop using. Then I was taken back to the other side of town to my secured apartment. After that I had no reason to go back to that side of town to see anymore.

There was another place Rod said he wanted to show me. It was a penthouse apartment. The place was very nice, although it looked like no one had lived there for a while. He said when the lease was up in the apartment. I was staying in I could move into the penthouse. I asked who lived there. He said an old friend, but the friend left town and wasn't coming back so he could sell it, rent it or do whatever with it. I asked about the furniture and stuff left. He said he had to have it cleaned out and he already had someone to take care of all that. Of course I wanted it. It was fabulous.

Chapter 25

I Got All My Sisters With Me

I knew very few people in Cleveland. One was my friend Diamond's grandmother, "Granny" who was as young at heart as we were. Granny frequented Alabama so connecting with someone familiar was comforting to have. Not only that but "Diamond would be visiting Cleveland more often now that I was there. Rod's niece Carly was coming to visit us soon, I also had another friend from high school who had family in Cleveland that was coming to visit. Once again, the music was painting my story for me because "We Are Family," by Sister Sledge was at the top of the music charts and I had my "sistas" with me. We were definitely about to have a family reunion. Rod was cool with my girls coming to visit after all, they kept me occupied and less likely to get homesick for Alabama.

Chapter 26

Friends or Foes?

Then there was the couple that Rod was friends with, or as he would say, "they were associates." The husband was called Crosstie. The wife's name was Londa. Londa was the only person from Cleveland that I can say actually visited my apartment and that was fewer times than I have fingers and not thumbs. Her husband Crosstie was around the stores a lot and worked for Rod. One of the stores was near where they lived. Of course, I didn't trust anyone and kept everyone eating out of a long handle spoon, which really proved to be for the best.

The associates, Crosstie and his wife Londa owned pit bull dogs and as a friendly gesture gave one to Rod for me. He asked if I wanted to keep it. It had all the necessary vaccinations and had pedigree documents. Rod said I could keep it at his other house, where I stayed when I would come to visit Rod early on before moving to Cleveland. Rod said because it was just a puppy I could keep it at the apartment for a while. It was so adorable and cute. Until one day I went to feed it after having him for about 3 months and he started growling at me and I felt really intimidated. I didn't know what was wrong with him, but he wasn't going to bite the hand that fed him because that hand was mine. Rod said I wasn't feeding it enough, which was why he was growling. I didn't care how valuable he was; he needed to find a new home right away. I'd found out from Londa that it came from a line of champion fighters which was something I'd never known anything about or desired to engage in.

Going out to a gathering for a Labor Day celebration with a rather large group of people at the Ranch was going to be a really "goodtime". It turned out to be the day I was introduced to the most disgusting, barbaric form of entertainment I had ever encountered. Seeing these pit bulls viciously attack one another and wrestle each other like men was not at all entertaining to me. It was horrific and insane. I wasn't about that foolishness. I realized right then and there that I had made the right decision in getting rid of the dog. I was not about to live with placating an animal that I was feeding and taking care of every day. When I look back at the situation, I'd determined that men are much like the animals they choose. Still there was much fun to be had at the ranch that day. Horseback riding was comical; cowboy hats were in and seeing them worn cocked to the side as some of the guys straddled their horses was quite funny. It was a day filled with laughter, especially when one of the horses didn't like its rider and as we're just trotting along a trail, this horse picked up speed and ran under a low branch with this guy, as if he had planned it. The horse knocked the rider off his back to the ground and then kept trotting back to the area we had started from. The guy had to ride back on the back of someone else's horse. It was a day intended for fun and entertainment. All's well that ends well, Right? Except for as we were leaving the Ranch, some in cars, some vans, and some motorcycles; and yes, we all had sufficient libations for the occasion. The guys on the motorcycles were always feeling the most uninhibited. They took off full throttle ahead of everyone else and as we veered around a curve to a fork in the street with a line of stores to the

Janet Evans

right, one guy lost control of his bike and met head on with the brick store front and was killed. My day was filled with observations and lessons. That day my desire for bikes went down to zero in just that second.

Chapter 27

The Visit I Should Have Expected

Now that I'd been in Cleveland for a while and had been back and forth to Alabama, guess who's coming to visit? My Mom was coming along with her friend to check out how I'm living for herself. She recognized I wasn't being held against my will or lacking anything and being treated well, so she left after a couple of days without dragging me back to Alabama. Rod was very clear about one thing from the very start. He'd send me home happy and safe like he found me if I ever decided I wanted to go but he was going to make sure I never wanted to. After Rod expressed that to my Mom, it gave her some peace of mind and she and her friend left me in Cleveland without much of a fight. She made it clear, I could always come home and that Rickey was coming to visit so they would be keeping a check on me. I talked to Rickey often and was looking forward to his visit the upcoming year. Jumping over that hurdle really helped Cleveland to start feeling more like home. My only obstacle now was being a Southern girl still trying to adjust to the upcoming winter months, although there was not much difference in Michigan and Ohio's cold air off the lakes that surround them. Neither of them was as comfortable as the mild short winters that the southern girl enjoyed. I focused on shopping, getting my apartment more winter friendly

Janet Evans

and without doing too much because I was contemplating the move to the penthouse and what I would do decorating it. I was looking forward to life getting better.

Chapter 28

Foe Confirmed

There was the day Londa showed up at my apartment for a visit after us discussing her stopping by several times before. She was about seven years older than me and was pregnant with Crosstie's 3rd child. He hadn't long been released from prison for(trafficking) and during one of their visits she must have conceived. Rod had been a great source of provision for them during Crosstie's time down. She often referred to all the help and how much they appreciated all Rod had done for them. Although I spent some time around Londa, it was all rather casual, at the store, dropping off merchandise for the store or waiting for them to get to the store. Londa started getting friendlier and wanting to hang out with me more. We had been to their apartment on a few occasions for one reason or the other. Visiting my apartment was not a common occurrence. Since Rod was not pulling my coat tail, so to speak, I allowed her to visit. I really didn't know what I was dealing with until the day she showed up for a brief visit.

Londa only stayed a short time. It was just a casual girl chat. She asked about Rod's whereabouts. I said out working. She remarked that Rod seemed so much happier since we were together and how close he and Crosstie were. Yet I knew Rod didn't really trust that closeness, not the way she was describing it. She asked if she could use the restroom before she left; being pregnant, she had to go all the time with the baby getting close to delivery. Since I had never been pregnant, I thought it made perfectly good sense to me. I directed her to the hall bathroom. Once finished she didn't stay long at all. I escorted her out and got right back to what I was doing before she came. I was expecting Rod to come by before long.

When he came in he asked what I had been up to. I said nothing much. I then told him that Londa had stopped by for a minute. I then went to the kitchen to prepare us something to eat. While he walked back to the bedroom area, then when he came back down the hall and passed the bathroom, he turned the light on in the bathroom. He came back out and asked who else had been over? I said no one except Londa. Then he asked had I been cleaning the toilet today? Now I'm confused. That's when he called me to come take a look at the toilet. Londa had left the toilet seat up like guys do when they use the toilet. Then Rod said I see the game they're playing. I didn't understand why Londa would have had to let the seat up to use the toilet in the first place. I never go into anyone's restroom and lift the seat to use the toilet unless it's too filthy to sit on. My guest restroom was always clean because I rarely had guests.

I didn't get what Rod meant by "I see their game" until he explained that Londa and Crosstie had devised a plot. For one thing before I showed up apparently Rod was forking out more to help their family. Crosstie being locked up for some time and now a new baby being added to the two they already had meant they were expecting more substantial perks. If I was removed from the equation, the flow could turn back to their direction. Little did I know the seed had been planted that I had some interest in Crosstie by Londa. Certain moves had been made by them both to raise suspicions. I was not aware of the full ramifications of such a plot when dealing with people in "The Life."

Rod was not at all taking this attempt to discredit me as just an attempt to remove me as their nemesis. I was ready to confront the situation. Rod said he was going to take care of it. He explained that the plot was even deeper than just removing me. In "The Life," if you want to mess with a man's mind, use his woman as a distraction. He will be off balance in handling his business which could be detrimental. These types of games were not to be taken lightly. Just like the puppy they had given me that I got rid of because it growled at me, never bite the hand that feeds you. At this point I was starting to understand that this arena is not as harmless as I viewed it. I mean, I was still stuck on Rod having something so urgent he had to miss his brother's funeral. With all this going on my fairytale was turning into a mystery novel. Especially when a week later, Rod and I were going out, I got in the car and there was a box in the back seat. "That's a new baby crib," he says. "We're dropping it off at Crosstie and Londa's for the baby." Of course, my question was why? After they were trying to cause us trouble, why do anything else for them. Once again Rod's answer left me baffled. "No, you don't change anything when people think they are crossing you. You should act as if nothing has changed. Seasons change and things are about to change with it. They'll need the bed cause he won't be able to hold the baby." Ok, so I was not going to ask what that meant. Yes, the Bad Girl wanted revenge, but that answer could mean something extreme. I thought Crosstie might be headed back to jail.

I've noticed that Rod seems busier than usual lately. He seemed to be sleeping less and was not as relaxed as before. Then

Janet Evans

one morning he came by with an uneasy disposition. Something that I was not accustomed to seeing on him. It was as if he wanted to pick a fight. I'm trying to figure out what's up. When a few heated words passed and when I looked as he turned his face towards me. I see something that I'd never seen before in my life, at least not outside of a horror movie. This man's face had taken on an entirely different configuration and even his complexion from brown to greyish. If I had never seen a demon in my life, I had just seen one manifest itself right in my presence. The disfiguration of his entire head frightened me so badly. It was as if my heart stopped beating. Then as quickly as it manifested itself, it retreated. Then he said, "Look, things around here are about to get complicated. I need you to go to Alabama for a while." Well, I was trying to contain myself without freaking out. He said you need to pack your things and get on a plane out of here. Call and book a flight today. I wanted to act as if I wanted to know why, but the truth was he didn't just see what I saw and there was no way at this point staying was on my mind. I called my Mom and said I'm coming to Alabama and was on a flight out the next morning.

No way could I tell Rod what had just been revealed to me. I was too afraid to say anything. Who was this man that I had regarded as the closest thing to my Guardian Angel? Now he seems to have transformed into Lucifer at least to anyone crossing him. I did understand that all the contemplating on the subject needed to be done once my feet hit Alabama soil. Still not knowing what was transpiring in Cleveland, he sent me back to Alabama ahead of him and said he'd be coming later in the week. He said, "I'll explain things then." I had no idea a murder was about to take place and another murder was about to follow. The "Bad Girl" was about to find out just how bad of company she had been keeping.

BAD GIRL 2
VIRTUOUS WOMAN
Chapter 29

Now that I'm back home in Alabama, I am feeling much more at ease. The unexplained drama that was left over 700 miles behind me in Cleveland was just where I wanted it. Even as I tried to explain away the encounter that I'd seen with my own eyes the week before when Rod's face transformed into a demon right before my very eyes. It's funny the things we will try to rationally explain away when we love someone, even after God has revealed to us the nefarious nature of a person. We sometimes tend to exculpate them based on our emotional ties.

I met with Rod once he arrived in Alabama. After all he'd shown me so much gentleness and care, I would be the last one to identify him as a danger. When he arrived in town, he had a friend from Cleveland with him. One that I had met and had been in his company several times before, a very attractive man with striking light brown eyes. Thomas was not someone who I considered a close associate of Rods. So for him to have brought him to Alabama and especially to his parent's house was a little strange. Yet at that time, I wasn't feeling as though I knew anything about what's going on at all. Once I met up with Rod at his parent's house, I entered the foyer area and saw this Louis Vuitton luggage sitting on the floor. It was very nice, so it grabbed my attention. As I walked past it, I commented, "Nice set of luggage." "Rod said, "It's Thomas's." Immediately I heard a voice speak to me saying, "He won't make it back to Cleveland alive." I was shocked! The voice was very calm and peaceable. I walked to the back room where Thomas and Carly, Rod's niece were sitting. Still stunned by what I had just heard, when asked if I'd like a drink? I answered yes right away, still contemplating if the voice was referring to Rod or Thomas. By the time I got the drink it was as if I knew it was Thomas because I could still see the luggage in my mind. After an hour or so, as I was preparing to go home, Rod and I walked out to discuss getting together later. He said he would pick me up at a set time so I went to regroup. I noticed that there was still this uncomfortable edge about him. He said he needed to explain why he needed me to come to Alabama and that he probably wasn't going back to Cleveland right away.

That evening he picked me up and we went to a hotel outside of Birmingham. Once we settled in he began to explain why me leaving Cleveland so abruptly was the best way for him to keep me safe. That he really loved me and wouldn't do anything to hurt me or allow anyone else to hurt me either. That was why he felt it best for me to leave Cleveland. When I ask, "Why are you not just telling me what's really going on?" He said, "I've always kept you safe away from "The Life" because I understand what this is all about and the truth of the matter is, I'd rather shovel sh-t. (manure) up to my neck for the rest of my life than to be in what I'm in. Now I think I'm starting to get the picture and I don't like what I see being painted. I didn't know how deep this was nor did I want to. I never even asked about the things that I had left behind in Cleveland in my apartment after that statement. Nor did I mention to him anything that I had experienced relating to seeing the demon manifest or hearing the voice say that Thomas wouldn't make it back to Cleveland alive. Nor did he just come out and say I'm in the Mafia.

It wasn't uncommon for him to have a weapon with him because he carried large sums of cash. Yet this particular night he has two guns in the briefcase that he laid on the table. Rod said he had to take care of some business over the next couple of days and would let me know his plans once he finished getting it straightened out. I felt as though I had just been told something that I really didn't want to know, although I didn't know what it was exactly that I had just been told. It was as if a story line from a movie with lots of plots and unexpected turns were being played out. I knew I hadn't been to a casting call, yet the drama seemed to only be beginning. Like it or not, I'd been given a script, even if only as an extra.

Since I'd not been alone with Rod since leaving Cleveland and seen the manifestation of the demon in him, for the first time I'm uneasy being alone with him. His persona had changed and was putting off a disturbing vibe. I'm wondering if we're safe at that very moment. Thoughts of the time he disappeared and hadn't shown up for his own brother's funeral were again at the forefront of my mind. When I mentioned us returning to Cleveland, I was told it was better for me to stay in Alabama. I acted as though I was disappointed to hear it. The truth was as much as I loved him, I had come to the realization Rod was not the guardian angel I'd made him out to be. Rather one that had disguised himself as an Angel of Light. He said he was headed to California and would send for me later. I noticed he had a bag in the briefcase that looked like a bag he carried jewelry in. He reached for it and said I have something for you. I want you to hold on to it for me until I see you again. I was hoping he wasn't about to ask me to marry him. Then he pulled out a diamond engagement ring and put it on my finger. He didn't ask me to marry him; he just said I'll always love you. It was a simple solitaire that I didn't particularly think was of any great value (which later proved to be a misconception on my part), but the fact that he was giving me a ring was special. I figured that it was just a precursor to something much bigger to come.

After staying the night at the hotel the next day he dropped me off at home and said he'd call later that evening. No call came that evening or the next day. I was visiting my friend Diamond, who visited her granny and me while I was in Cleveland. She lived very close to a wooded area near the back of a local hospital. We noticed the sound of sirens, police cars and helicopters. Then it was about the time of the evening news when a special news break came on the TV. Announcing that they were at the scene of what they described as a horrific murder and the location was right at Diamond's front door. The news report said that they knew that the victim was not local but was a black male from Cleveland Ohio. They could not release any more information pending family notification.

Then one report said that they knew that the victim also had been killed execution style with the head nearly decapitated and had been cut from ear to ear. Diamond and I both were in total shock. It was as if we were both grasping for the same breath of air. Not knowing if it was Rod that had been murdered or maybe Thomas or maybe even someone else. All I could think of was the fact that I had heard the voice speak to me saying that Thomas would not make it back to Cleveland alive. In a panic, I called Rod's parent's house to see if his niece Carly could give me better details. There was no answer and the phone was busy. What was reported next was that a man had walked down the street to the police station holding a shotgun and turned himself in to the police. Stating he had killed the man they found in the woods behind the hospital in self-defense and he too was from Cleveland, Ohio. As the story continued to play out, it was reported that Thomas had followed Rod to Alabama with the intent to kill him. That Thomas had lured him into the woods under the pretense of them meeting someone there but then attacked Rod. Rod having been in Special Forces had been trained to kill and disarmed Thomas and slew him.

It was not by any means a relief to know that Thomas was dead and that Rod had taken his life. The description of the brutal murder scene frightened me more than anything. If there had been just a shooting death, I felt I could have taken it better. Knowing that Rod could physically take a knife and cut Thomas's throat from ear to ear, nearly decapitating him, sent me into an unimaginable state of shock. I felt as though they both were dead because the image of this kind gentleman that I had known in Rod had just been murdered along with Thomas. I really was in fear for my life because how did I know who was meeting them in the woods or why they were meeting them there.

How was I supposed to know if others had followed Rod to Alabama? The fact that I didn't know what was really going on frightened me the most. I was literally sick on the stomach. I remembered Rod saying that he was part of Special Forces and was a Green Beret as he showed me different Awards, Purple Heart and medals. I guess the training that he spoke of saying the US Government trained them to kill was true and certainly effective. When he spoke of the military experiences, I kinda took it too lightly, thinking he was too young to have really been too involved in Special Forces. Although I saw the Green Beret and bars, killing people was too far out of character for this gentle man. I needed answers and the only person I felt comfortable talking to would be my friend Carly, Rod's niece who had introduced us. It was urgent that I speak with her. I didn't want to go to his parent's house where she was. Just in case there were investigators there asking questions. I thought it was best that I just lay low. I didn't want to stay at my mother's house just in case there was anybody wanting to question me in regard to anything concerning the case. I didn't want anyone who might be looking to harm me to find me at my mom's house. If there was anything else coming down the tube it would have to find me somewhere else. I moved around a lot for the next couple of weeks. There was no word from Rod. He was in the city jail and being process to the county.

Chapter 30

The Plot Thickens

As the weeks went by; newspaper reports came out from the police investigations. Not only was Thomas dead but Cleveland had issued an arrest warrant for Rod as well. For the murder of Crosstie. Apparently, Crosstie had been killed a few days after I left Cleveland. The paper also stated that he had been charged with a murder several years before of a woman that he had dated. The report also stated that the woman he killed had been dead in the penthouse apartment for a few days and that he had been there in the apartment with the corpse over 24 hours before leaving. I realize that the penthouse was more than likely the one he was offering me to move into. No wonder it looked as though no one had lived in it for some time and had the appearance of someone not moving out but just leaving.

Later another newspaper article that was written about the incident mentioned the female victim's name. Rod had actually mentioned that name before in conversation. Of course, I wondered what in the world could have provoked him to do something like that to a woman? What was all the killing and secrecy? Who were these people and what was the next unexpected fallout? Even though Rod had reassured me that he had kept me away from "the life," how could I trust that when "the life" had followed me home to Alabama. It had also resulted in the death of two individuals that I had associated with for a period of time and landed Rod in jail. I had to wonder if I was being watched and if I might be thought to have known something that I didn't know. One question that I needed answered had gotten answered. That was if the demon that I saw manifested on Rod was real? The answer proved to be yes and alive and in full operation. How many times a day did I ask myself, how could someone that treated me with all the respect, adoration and tenderness, that many women had never experienced be wrapped up in a killer? It sent chills down my spine. Yet, I loved him, at least the man I knew.

During the time period of waiting for Rod to contact me I received a call from a woman. This woman called my apartment where my cousin answered and gave her the number where I was. When this lady got me to the phone she asked if I could give a message to a guy by a name that I was not familiar with. I said no I don't know him. I said she had contacted the wrong person. For one thing, this woman's voice nor the accent was not at all familiar to me. She spoke with an Italian accent. She said, "No, you are Janet Evans," and then she quoted the address where I lived in Cleveland. "Yes, I do have the right person," she said. "I want you to deliver this message to (alias name of the person that she mentioned earlier)." Once she gave me the message, I knew it had to be for Rod even though I didn't recognize the name. That was the end of her conversation.

By the following week they had transferred Roc down to the county jail. That was my opportunity to go visit him face-to-face. I needed to get some answers and deliver the message that the woman had given me. This was one of the most unnerving situations I had ever encountered. But I needed to see him, not only to see his physical being but also to see if there was anything else I needed to know in regards to my own safety. I had never been to visit anyone in jail; it was foreign to me. Seeing him behind bars was surreal. He reassured me that I was in no danger. The one thing I did want an answer to was how he could have murdered a woman he had dated. For some reason I could not bring myself to ask the question. I guess I realized this was not a question that he wanted to discuss from behind bars. Much to my surprise, Rod made a statement that answered any questions I had regarding all the murders he had committed. When he said to me, "One thing I want you to know is this. I have never killed anyone that didn't deserve to die." There was nothing much to be said behind that statement.

He then followed with another statement that was just as baffling, "I will be out in the year of the monkey." I had no idea what that was supposed to mean. At least not at that particular time. As I left that visit, I felt that was the last time we would see each other for quite a while, and it was. Although it was bittersweet, I was ready to be as far removed from the drama as possible. All Rod could say was remember what I've told you and take care of yourself. Then life moved on. Then one day I was out at a Chinese Restaurant with a friend for lunch. I noticed the placemat the waitress place in front of me had a Chinese Calendar that gave a listing for the year of the Dog, Rat, Tiger, Monkey, etc. I was shocked. I had never noticed anything regarding the Chinese Calendar, it was the year of the Dog and according to the calendar he would be out in three years. True enough that year he was released just as he said he would be.

Chapter 31

Reconstruction Phase

I was home for 2 months; I began looking for a job. I applied at the local hospital where I had been a Candy Striper when I was in high school and where Thomas's body had been found in the woods. I was hired in the laboratory once again as a phlebotomist. Working in the lab there was great. I soon moved into a nice apartment in an area not too far from my job. Everything is now back to normal. Working and going out with my friends enjoying the single life again. One thing that I wasn't quite ready for was getting back into the dating scene. My relationship with Rod had left me with the emotional feelings of being widowed or divorced and not seeing it coming. Yet being young it didn't take me long to readjust.

Chapter 32

Jungle Fever

About 6 months later I was out with my girlfriend Diamond at a club, downtown Birmingham when I was approached by a handsome man who was very well-dressed. He grabbed my attention when he began to speak to me. He had a very strong accent that sparked my curiosity. Which led me to engage him in further conversation. I asked him where he was from. I was quite surprised when he informed me that he was from Nigeria. For one thing I had always been under the impression that for the most part, Africans, at least those that I had come in contact with were short in stature and not as well put together as this guy. Which only added to the curiosity. After he asked for my phone number and if he could see me again. I couldn't refuse finding out more about his story. We started dating. It was fun, interesting, and alluring. I just couldn't really understand a lot of what I assumed to be his customs when it came to dating. He never really wanted to go out to the club. He only wanted to spend time at his place and around his friends. Then I began to realize these were a player's moves and had nothing to do with culture. So after only 3 months of dating what happens? The girl who was told that she had endometriosis and couldn't get pregnant was pregnant. Now my life is about to take another turn. This man is in college completing his master's degree and it won't be very long before he's finished

Janet Evans

and probably ready to go back to Nigeria. I am still emotionally unattached. Yet I'm about to have a child with this man and I'm not sure he's really into me enough to marry me either. The only thing I know to do is what I've always done and that is, just keep it moving one way or the other.

It's true what they say a man can make a woman be the sweetest woman he's ever known or the meanest woman he'll ever know. Of course my guy chose the latter. Now he starts talking about going back to Nigeria for the Christmas holiday. How do I know if he's going to come back really. So, what does a sister do? She goes to have him put on child support even before the child is born. How does she do that? Well, she did. After that there was no sign of him for the duration of the pregnancy. I gave birth to a beautiful Nigerian Princess in July. It was October in the courtroom before he ever laid eyes on her. By December we had reconciled our differences and when he presented the subject of marriage I declined. I knew neither of us was in love with each other. Not only that I believed he only had the capacity to be self-serving and that characteristic would only fuel another Maggie & Loundry relationship. I felt as though I had already taken one of those wooden nickels that Rod had warned me about. I found that my suspicions were right. H was messing with another woman while I was pregnant and I wasn't about to take another wooden nickel, not even under the auspices of marriage, not from the same man. Now the bad girl is really coming to the forefront and the good girl is hidden somewhere deep in the shadows. I had not felt so betrayed or wounded since I was 13 years old after finding out that my dad was getting married and had not told me or my brother, nor invited us to the wedding. So now this man has really wounded the good girl again. Since he was my child's dad, I had to tolerate this hurt and act as if it didn't tear my heart apart, not for myself but for the sake of my child.

How much pain does a woman bear for the sake of a child, and not only in childbirth? After getting past all of the hurt moving, forward is the only thing to do. He gave me a few thousand dollars, started to pay child support, gave me a car and he moved on traveling from place to place and showing up at will. No emotional support, soon no child support or any other kind of support. Thank God for moms. We will always come to help meet the needs of our children. As I continued to work my mom and my brother Rickey would help take care of my daughter.

Finally, I started adjusting to working and carrying financial responsibility for both myself and my child. Then life happened. Another unexpected chain of events occurred. The word began to circulate that the hospital I was working at was to be sold. No one knew exactly how long it would be, but it was official. That's when I decided to go to KeepSake Jeweler to get the last ring Rod had given me appraised. I was shocked to find out it was valued at close to $5000. So that was some cushion for me. Yet some people had worked there for 30 years were about to lose their jobs. Some people were actually crying tears because they had invested their whole lives into being a part of an establishment that only valued them as far as the dollar would extend them to. Me being a newcomer my job was definitely on the chopping block. I was being laid off for the first time ever. That was bad but not devastating for me. I felt that I could get another job really soon and not only that, but I could also take the layoff and spend time with my daughter. So, that news wasn't as devastating to me, not as much as the news I was about to receive. This news would change the course of my life in a way I could have never imagined. It was more devastating than all the heartbreaks I had ever experienced combined.

Chapter 33

The Same Voice Speaks

I'm in my apartment with my daughter, just having a normal cleaning day and relaxing. When the doorbell rings, it's my brother Rickey stopping by. He came over to hang out so of course I gave him the sofa no problem. Later on that evening as I was walking through the living room from the kitchen going back to my room, I heard a voice speaking to me as I passed by my brother lying on the sofa taking a nap. It was one I had heard before. It was the same voice that had spoken to me concerning Thomas not making it back to Cleveland alive. The voice said, "He won't be here long." I stopped and looked at him for more than a minute and tried to just shake it off, although I knew what I heard was God's Spirit speaking to me. Although my spirit knew it was real, my flesh was in total rejection. I loved my brother. We were like twins. Eleven months apart, we were all each other had. We didn't always agree, but I loved him dearly. I needed him to be in my daughter's life. Especially since her dad wasn't playing a consistent role of a father. A couple of months passed, and I was still working at the hospital. They had not announced the layoff of the lab personnel yet. It was a Sunday evening and I had just gotten off work about 3 that afternoon. When I went to my mother's house to meet with Rickey because he would keep my daughter until I made it home from work to pick her up from my mother's house. My mother had to leave for work 30 minutes earlier before I got off work for her to be to work on time at 3p.m. It only took me about 10 minutes to get to my mother's house from work. It was a beautiful September day, and my plans were to take my daughter to the park once I went home, showered, and put on some more clothes. When I pulled up that day in front of my mother's house Rickey was outside in the yard playing with my daughter. When I walked up I asked him what he was about to do. He seemed to be in a bit of a hurry. His countenance had a strange grey cast, something that was so obvious to me.

He said he was going to talk to this guy that was from our neighborhood because the guy was upset with him and threatened him, telling him to stay away from 54th Street, where they both were selling marijuana and some pills from this girl's house. Rickey said that the guy had not long left my mother's house just as she was getting ready to leave for work. He also said that the guy had a gun on him, but he was going to go and talk to him. I told him to be careful because you can't really reason with fools. I knew the guy personally just the year before he and I had done a business deal and had traveled to New York. He really wanted a relationship with me, something that I was totally not interested in because he was a Muslim and already had a wife. According to him, his beliefs allowed him to have as many wives as he could afford. I had refused his offer. I returned from New York a day or so before him. He found me at the club with my best friend Diamond. I was talking to a guy when he walked up and he asked me to step outside so that he could show me what he brought back from New York. Before we left to go to New York he had a large amount of women's clothing for sale. They were silk dresses and a couple of Albert

Janet Evans

Napone women's suits. I had chosen a couple of silk dresses and the suits. I told him I could not pay him for them until I got back from New York. He had no hesitation about letting me get them until I got back. He knew my money was good. But once I was back and he saw me at the club talking to this guy at the bar he comes over to me and says, "I want to see you outside." I told my friend Diamond to come let's walk outside and see what he was talking about. Once we were outside, he started to question me about the guy that I was talking to at the bar. I told him it really wasn't his business. We were strictly business and that was the way I wanted to keep it. But he started to act belligerent. He had a partner with him and his partner said to him, "Man, why are you acting like that with this lady? She's not your woman."

By then my girl Diamond and I had decided we might have to go for what we know, so I had already pulled off one of my six-inch heels ready to plug him in the eye with it if it was going to have to be something. His partner told him to come on, let's go. He seemed to have calmed down and then left with his partner. I knew he was emotionally unstable and possessive.

I told Rickey to be careful. He looked back at me as he walked away. The grayish complexion that seemed to have covered his countenance lingered in my mind. I stopped at my girl Diamond's house on my way home to see if she was going to go to the park. I was about to go change clothes. The children were playing so well together that she told me to just run home and change and let them continue to play until I got back. She had a son a month older than my daughter and we often took them to the park together. I agreed and ran home to shower and change. Once I got to my apartment, for some reason I just couldn't get myself together. It was as if I was just walking in circles. My thoughts were on the conversation that I just had with my brother and the grey complexion of his countenance that greatly disturbed me. By the time I got out of the shower the phone was ringing. It was my girlfriend Diamond telling me that I needed to go quickly to the hospital where I had just gotten off work; because someone had just said Rickey had been shot and was in the emergency room. I remember my heart was pounding so fast because at that very moment, I was standing right next to the sofa where Rickey had last laid. When I had heard the voice of the Spirit saying to me, "He won't be here long," just a couple of months before.

I threw my clothes on as fast as possible. I rushed to the hospital emergency room. Because I worked there, I went straight back to the trauma area where they were working on Ricky. They knew he was my brother and didn't want to let me get any closer to see what was going on. I said to them I have to see my brother. They let me come closer. They were talking, saying they couldn't stop the bleeding.

They had ordered more units of blood. They were getting ready to take him up to surgery. I was able to speak with him. As he lay on the table in the trauma room he was saying, "I'm not ready to die! Don't let me die!" As I stood next to him, I could see the gunshot wound and all the blood that he was losing even though they had already given him 8 units of blood at that time, and it was not holding. I nearly passed out at that point, but I regained my strength because I didn't want to leave him and I knew they were about to take him to surgery. My mom had been notified but she had not reached the hospital yet. I walked along beside him on the stretcher all the way to the operating room doors. I remember saying to him, "I told you he was a fool; you can't talk to fools." Then he looked at me and said with a slight grin on his face, "Don't worry about me

Janet Evans

Jan. I'm going to be alright." And just this calm peaceful voice came over him and he said it again, "I'm going to be alright." Then his last words to me were, "He did me wrong." They swiftly pushed him through the door to surgery. He never spoke to me again. By the time my mom arrived he was already back in surgery; I was the last one to talk to him. By the time my dad and stepmom got there we were all just sitting in the waiting room waiting for them to bring him out to a room. After surgery they placed him in a room, but he never really came out of surgery. The next morning, they told us he was only breathing by the machine and there was nothing that they could do. He had lost too much blood. My baby brother was gone. Nothing on earth could have broken our bond but death. My Irish twin that I had shared this life with left me here to deal with life without him. I felt as though someone had stabbed me in the heart and was twisting the knife. The murderer was on the loose trying to evade law enforcers. He finally turned himself in after getting a lawyer to represent him.

My poor mom had just lost her youngest child and her only son. It was one of the darkest times of my life and it was a season that only God could get us through. And if that wasn't enough. I remember us going to the funeral home to prepare the body for burial. Oddly enough the funeral home director was a Pastor whose church I had recently visited. I was so impressed with his delivery of the word. So much so that I had determined that I would go back to visit again and maybe even make it my home Church. Until the evening we went in to meet with him for the funeral arrangements. He informed us that my brother was tall and would need an extra-long casket. He had measured him at about 6 ft 7". When we went back to see the body, I noticed something unusual. My brother's feet were bent downward and not at all in the position that they were in at the hospital when he died. At the hospital they had placed a sponge block at the end of the bed, so his feet were pointed straight up. What I recognized was that they had broken the bone in his foot and extended his foot outward and downward to measure him at another length to charge for an extra-long casket. This sent me into an absolute rage. I told that funeral director/ pastor exactly what I thought of him being a con man and a greedy perpetrator. That I was not coming back to his church because he really couldn't teach me anything about God being the phony that he was. And a few other choice words that my dad had to call me down on, which I had a whole lot of anger toward him as well. I felt as though he had thrown my brother to the wolves by not being there to really father his oldest son. My respect level for men was pretty much at an all-time low. After discovering the heinous act of desecration of Rickey's body to gain money for an extra-long casket. He had to be reported to the board of Mortuary Services of Alabama. The director of the board was someone that my mother knew personally. He actually stepped in and took it from there. My mother didn't want to issue a lawsuit against them because they were a new black owned and operated business in the community.

The board informed her she had every right to do so and could definitely be awarded compensation for her pain and suffering behind this funeral home's actions. We proceeded with allowing them to carry out the services, and of course, they did an excellent job.

That's why as people of God, we must learn that we must deal fairly with people. God is always watching our character. We got through the burial, but life was not at all the same.

Chapter 34

Reap What You Sow or Karma

Not long after the burial we had some unexpected visitors. Two men showed up at my Mom's house. They said they knew Rickey and that they came to let us know that they would take care of the situation and bring us the finger that had pulled the trigger that took his life. The guy that took his life was still out on bond at that time. I guess we were both shocked at their suggestion. My reply was, "No, let him live because if you kill him, his suffering will be over. Death is too good for him." That statement held true because about a year or so later the guy that killed Rickey, his sister went to the police station and placed a restraining order of protection against her husband. As she left the police station and got into her car, her husband pulled his car in front of hers and blocked her in at the police station. He got out of his car, went to her car, shot her in the head, killing her. He then turned the gun on himself and killed himself. It's amazing how life is. Vengeance still belongs to God. Not that I was glad that it happened to his sister, but I would be lying if I did not say I was glad that I allowed him to live. He now would have to see and feel exactly what it felt like for someone to take your sibling's life. Only there was nothing that he could do about it because the brother-in-law took his own life and left no room for vengeance for him.

Now my brother had a girlfriend that he was seeing before his death. She and I had bonded since his death. The bonds of mutual loss can turn out to be stronger than blood. Marie's two girls and my daughter bonded like sisters, just as Marie and myself. The other thing we had in common was getting high. So we dedicated ourselves to having each other back. After Rickey's death she eventually went back to her girl's Dad. They married within the following year. We were all like family. One night Maria and I left my apartment with the girls in the car with us. We were headed to her apartment, which was about 8 miles apart. We were driving Ricky's old car, a Lincoln Continental. I don't know why the brakes totally failed and the horn on the car would not blow. We had to pass through at least 6 busy intersections where traffic lights were. With absolutely no brakes the car was moving at a pace of about 35 to 45 miles an hour at times. Without a horn to even alert other cars there was anything wrong. Pushing on the emergency brakes did not stop or slow the pace of the car. My baby sensing something was very wrong began to cry My Janet!!! My Janet from the rear seat. At one point out of pure desperation I even opened the door to stick my foot out on the pavement to try to slow the pace of the car. Realizing that was not the answer, I retrieved my foot without any damage. We approached an intersection that is always busy and the traffic light on our side had turned red. Yet the traffic on the other side that had the right of way was green. Those cars stood still as if there was a force standing in front of them. There is no doubt in my mind that the angels of God had encamped about us. Delivering us from destruction and we were in amazement. Everybody knows that in Birmingham the traffic is not standing still at a green light. We traveled through these lights one after the other without incident. I counted at least eight streets until we finally came to an apartment complex that had a row of tall shrubberies and was slightly uphill, so I

Janet Evans

ran the car into the bushes. We all came out without a scratch! Did I say GOD is real? Maria and I remembered the night of this incident for many years. Recognizing the only explanation for what happened was that we had witnessed a miracle.

Chapter 35

Once Again, the Roaring Lion Seeks Whom He May Devour

Maybe just about a month before Ricky was murdered, I had met a man, who in so many ways reminded me of my brother Ricky. Tall, slim, attractive, well-dressed, and seemingly very intelligent. Initially, my thoughts were not to get involved. This guy was about ten years my senior and had previously been in the military and also work for the railroad company. The problem was he no longer did either. He had turned to the streets as a hustler. Good Girls like Bad Boys if you didn't know. His game was good, but his drug habit was even stronger. Of course the extent of it was not made known to me at that time. I was still involved myself, but my drug of choice was marijuana.

Snorting cocaine never really did much for me. I could take it or leave it. It was most definitely a product that I had many reservations about after the relationship with Rod was over. The cost of it was too high and its effects were too low to invest in regularly. Yet this was the drug of choice for this man. He often traveled across the country. When he was in town he and I spent time together. He was a big spender and loved expensive things. The problem was he spent money like there was no tomorrow. Then when tomorrow came there was no money to spend. Which was not a recipe for stability. But it did fulfill

Janet Evans

another nounscript that I was writing for myself. Remember a nounscript is a person, a place, or a thing used to compensate for a painful experience in a person's life.

During this process of meeting Greg, the hospital laid me off. They paid us a severance package and afterward, I drew unemployment compensation. Which enabled me to be home and enjoy my daughter. During the same time my mom was already in the process of moving out of Birmingham to Talladega County before my brother was murdered. On many weekends my daughter, who was my mom's only grandchild, went to spend time with her, which was a good thing for my mom as well. Greg invited me to New York for a weekend. It was a date that I was excited about and looking forward to. Little did I know that it would be a weekend that would affect my life for seven years to come. When I got to New York he picked me up at LaGuardia and brought me to the Hotel. Once I arrived the party was on. The booze, the weed, and the caine. The one thing I wasn't ready for was that he had a pipe. The very thing that Rod had warned me about earlier. Greg begins mixing the powder in water and with the test tube and fire. I knew then it was what was called freebasing. I really was uncomfortable with him doing it. Then he forcefully and repeatedly continued to push the pipe to my mouth saying just try it, inhale and hold it. I can honestly say I really wasn't a willing participant in this one. All my thoughts were of the things that Rod had warned me about. How women would be grossly taken advantage of when they'd become addicted to the pipe drug. I told Greg how uncomfortable I was with this pipe thing and didn't want it anymore. I became very agitated and angry with him. He backed off temporarily. I didn't know he was actually addicted or that he even smoked the pipe until we were in New York. He tried to act as if it was just a new thing and we were just trying it for fun. I later realized that was not the case for him. Before I could grasp the full situation, he and I had become so close. We shared so many good times together. He was always thinking ahead with future plans for us. Things like starting his own accounting business, he was a business major. Buying a home because of his military VA status. He wanted to continue to travel and have a family. He was good with my daughter and really liked spending time with us. He began taking us to visit his family -the grandmother who had raised him, and the aunt, his mother's sister and her husband, who were very instrumental in raising him. His mother left him with her mother before moving out west and starting another family with her new husband. Their relationship was quite strained. That's when I learned that he was broken and had been writing his own nounscripts for a long time. If I had only understood that two broken vessels put together does not necessarily make a whole. The brokenness I was still dealing with from my brother's murder was an ongoing nightmare. There were a few times I'd ran across his murderer in the neighborhood while he was out on bond before the trial. The loss of my brother caused such a vehement, heavy, cold, dark cloud that seemed to blanket my entire life. It seemed as though wherever I went death was following close after me. Many times, I wondered if I was next. Greg and I grew closer month by month. He knew he was not what I needed, just as I did, but we found ourselves falling in love. Yes, the girl that had no place for trusting a man had opened her heart to someone and thought love would this time be enough to conquer all our troubles. Things were going well. I felt as though I had found someone who loved me almost as much as Rod had. The relationship had grown from months to years, seemingly quickly. The problem was that the promises of the future growing brighter were not manifesting and the conspicuous nature of who Greg really was becoming clearer. He and I had been together for five years. I started to believe that he wanted to hold on to me by supplying drugs to keep me home and connected to him. Once I realized he really didn't want to give up the drugs, finally I got tired of him, the drugs and the promises of a normal life. That fifth year I prayed, "Lord, take this love away from me for this man please!" It was a long journey for the next two years until my uncle got sick, and I had to go back to LA to get him. It was my great escape. My daughter would stay with my Mom while I went to care for my Uncle. It's an enigma how life works, and every piece is important for our journey.

On my flight to LA there was the most beautiful man that I'd ever seen in the airport in ATL. He was so fine that even the men took notice of him. I know this because Greg was in ATL when my flight from Birmingham to LA had a brief layover there. Greg and one of his friends came to see me for food and drinks before my flight left. That's when Maurice walked into the restaurant and all eyes were on him, looking as if he'd just stepped off the runway of GQ Magazine. Tall, dark, fine, well dressed, and handsome. When Greg and his friend started to make comments about how that guy (Maurice) could get caught by them with the con- game and they could break him and take him to the bank and get all that gold he was wearing. I knew whatever they thought didn't matter. All I knew was that this was the best looking man I'd seen in a long time, if not in my life, and apparently so did everyone else in the airport that gave him a second and third look.

Soon it was time for me to board my flight to LA. Greg and I said our goodbyes and we agreed to talk later that evening once I got settled. Much to my surprise, as I boarded the flight and got comfortable sitting next to this nice Caucasian young man, in walks Maurice and sits right across the aisle from me and the other gentleman. The flight was not excessively crowded. As the flight went into progress the flight attendant asked passengers if they would like a movie and a drink. I said yes, I would like both and I handed her a $100 bill. She informed me that they didn't take large bills, so the man next to me said I'll buy it for her. By that time Maurice had already pulled out his money and said, "I'll take care of her," and said to me, "Why don't you come over and have a seat with me and watch the movie." Well of course that was the right move to make, and I made it without any hesitation. I thanked the gentleman next to me and moved across the aisle to engage in conversation with Maurice. He was heading to Los Angeles as well and found that he was originally from Tuscaloosa, Alabama. During our flight we talked a lot about why I was going there and where I'd be staying and how long I would be there. Once we arrived, he offered to have his friend drop me off. I declined the offer. Although we did exchange numbers and made plans for him to show me around while I was there. Ironically, he lived on Wilshire Boulevard not very far from my girlfriend's apartment on North Hamilton in Beverly Hills.

    Once I got there my job was to get my uncle to the Veteran's Hospital in Orange County and get him back to Alabama. Immediately I worked on the task at hand. The next morning I got him treated at the hospital. After he was given his medication, he was calm enough, so I placed him on a flight to Alabama. The problem was my uncle wanted his vehicle, which he had filled with all his personal goods, driven back to Alabama. This meant I had to have someone drive back with me to Alabama. I didn't tell Greg that I had already placed my uncle on the flight to Alabama, not for at least two weeks. When I did, he volunteered to get a flight to Los Angeles to help me drive back. Which was going to take another couple of weeks which was fine with me.

Janet Evans

When Maurice called asking if I would like to go out for brunch, I accepted his invitation. When he showed up my girlfriend was taken back. She wanted to know how in the world I had come across a man that fine that quick when she really hadn't seen one that fine and she had been in Los Angeles for 8 years. The next day that I was there he picked me up for a champagne brunch on Sunset Boulevard. Later that evening he invited me to the Speakeasy on Sunset. The women were so forward that one actually sent Maurice over a drink by the waitress. As the waitress pointed her out to him, he politely told the waitress to tell her, I have a date with me. I politely picked up the drink, smiled and drank it. We spent time at the beaches. He was a perfect gentleman. After having been under all the stress of dealing with Greg for five years this man was a breath of fresh air. God had finally answered my prayer. After spending time with Maurice in Los Angeles it only affirmed what I already knew which was my life should be going much better than what it was. Coming back to Alabama dealing with Greg was not something that I look forward to. Yet by now I'm missing my baby girl and I've got to get back home.

I knew I had to put some space between myself and Maurice in time for Greg to come and help me drive back. The day before leaving Maurice and I enjoyed ourselves to the fullest. And I prepared myself to come back to Alabama and start working diligently to end my relationship with Greg. Which I knew was going to be an ugly task, but it had to be done. My friend Dianne who was probably at least ten years older than me would often tell me Jan sometimes you have to ease your hand out of the lion's mouth, not snatch it out. She often shared advice as it related to relationships. She knew Greg and knew of his possessive nature toward me and my desire to rid myself of him.

Chapter 36

Not One but Two What?????

Greg arrived and as soon as he did we hit the road. I really did not want my girlfriends in LA to spend too much time talking with him. Knowing he would be cunningly trying to find out what I had been doing while I was there. We left immediately. We stopped all along the way having a great time. Stopping in Yuma and Old Tombstone, Arizona. Driving through the desert in 115 degrees heat, packing bags of ice on top of the engine under the hood, stopping in the daytime, sleeping and driving at night. Then on to visit his mom in El Paso, then friends in Houston then finally back to Alabama. Yet and still, nothing had changed with him. He still wanted his drugs and to drag me down with him. The difference now was that the thrill was gone. I knew he could tell nothing would ever be the same.

I had changed and started to become distant. At the same time he began to be extremely attentive and clingy. I even noticed him drinking ginseng teas and trying to get me to drink it as well. Not paying much attention as to why. But within 2 months back in Alabama, the most unexpected event came about. I was pregnant. One day after he woke up from taking a nap and came down the stairs. He said to me you know that you're pregnant and that you have two babies in you. I responded, "You are crazy." You need to stop getting high." Yet soon after the doctor confirmed it, yes, not only was I pregnant, but we were also having twins. It was just the incentive I needed to stop getting high. I couldn't believe that this was happening, Not at this time. Just as I was ready to walk away and never look back. Unbelievable!

I decided to endure the relationship until after the twins were born. Then another unexpected twist took place. Two months before the twins were born, Greg comes and tells me that he has just had a child by another woman. Which meant that while I was in LA, he had gotten her pregnant during that time. He thought he was telling me something that was going to really break my heart and that he was going to have to really try to make up for. Little did he know that was the best news I had heard in months.

I felt that was a good enough excuse for me to get rid of him forever. Yet, it took 18 months after the twins were born to break totally free. Please hear me people, ask yourself honestly before allowing yourself to fall in love with someone – is that person's faults and idiosyncrasy something you can tolerate for the rest of your life before you marry them or have children with them? Honestly, I am glad that the day we went to get married, which was even before I was pregnant with the twins. I heard the soft voice say, "No, don't do it." I then turned to Greg and said, "No, I can't." He was upset that we had gotten within the parking area of the building to get our license and blood test and I had changed my mind. Obviously, I had not always obeyed the voice of God. That was one time I am so glad that I did.

Please if you take nothing else away with you after reading this book. Remember this, the only reason God sets boundaries for us is because he really loves us so much and knows that when we do make bad decisions and cross those boundaries they will affect our lives, for the rest of our lives. When I was in my twenties and heard that statement, I would think to myself just because it happened to them doesn't mean it will happen to me. Anyway, I'll cross that bridge when I get to it. Believe me when I say staying inside GOD'S way of doing things can save you from a whole lotta drama and unnecessary heartaches. I learned that when I got to those bridges that I had to cross. The bridges were in need of repairs, down or were over seriously troubled waters and many times impossible to cross without the LORD'S help.

I wish I could have turned back the hands of time. Falling in love with Greg would be the one thing I wouldn't have allowed myself to do. People say you can't help who you fall in love with. I say you can by walking away before you do. Ask yourself realistic questions from the start, don't wait until you're too deep in, as I had done. Where would I be 10 years from now if I remained in the relationship? What would my life really be like If I stayed? And if the answer is bleak or disturbing just walk away from love.

One thing I know for sure, you can only make decisions for you no matter how much you may want better for others. Nevertheless, you owe it to yourself to make decisions that are going to give you the type of consequences that you want out of life. Not sure why while in my 20s I didn't like the term, "your actions have consequences." Maybe because I didn't like the idea of the consequences not being favorable or long-term. One thing Greg often said has proved to be true. Was that if I was

Janet Evans

to ever leave him, no one after him would have enough game to play me. That held true I had seen too much dealing with the con man. The uncontrolled drug use was more than I bargained for. Getting rid of Greg was the first solution.

Chapter 37

My Sister from Another Mother

After my travels to Los Angeles and sharing my adventure with my girl Marie, I believe it sparked a desire in her to travel. By then she and her husband had hit a hard spot and she had started hanging with a couple that lived near there recently relocated home. Me being pregnant had changed my partying to full time mothering. We were still close but not in the same circle. Marie decided to travel to Fort Worth, Texas with her new friend leaving her kids with her mom and their Dad. I had no idea she would stay gone for a year. During that time we had little communication. I knew something wasn't right. The devil had stepped in to destroy. When she finally came home to stay. She didn't go back to her husband but got involved with what I called a handsome demon. That had taken control of her life. Be careful young & beautiful everything that looks good is NOT at all what it appears to be at first sight. One day I run into the guy and Marie. He sends her to my car to tell me she and I can no longer hang out together. As she is facing me he is standing behind her waiting for her to give me the news. As she is delivering me the message, she's winking her eye at me to let me know he's put her up to it. I realized then he was a manipulative, dangerous individual. I just didn't know how she had gotten caught up with the demon, which proved to be exactly what he was. Marie had always proved to be a strong-minded person, well until she hooked up with Damon, the demon.

He was such an abusive man; he would physically beat her like a runaway slave. He even beat a couple of babies out of her. I'll never forget the day she told me that she had been hiding out for two months. Her mom had the kids although they were in school. This was Marie's attempt to break free of this monster. I went to visit her one day and she told me how she was at the grocery store and Damon, the demon had attacked her so viscously a man that never seen Damon or her before pulled out a gun and told Damon if he hit Marie one more time, he would blow his brains out right then and there. Of course, he was able to control himself then. The last time she told me that after returning from her 2 months of being MIA. Damon, the demon told her if she left him again he would kill her. She also said he meant it. She really thought he would do it. She insisted that we go buy film to take pictures with the new camera she had. So we did, take pictures of her and also of our kids.

Then when me and my kids were getting ready to leave, Maria said, "Jan you and I are closer than my natural sister and me. I want you to know I love you and these babies so much." I assured her we loved her and the girls too. She then said, "I know if I leave him again, he's going to kill me." I responded, "He looks better laying there in a box than you do. So get you a gun and protect yourself." But by the following Friday I got a call from my Mom saying she had just gotten a call from B'ham and Maria had been shot and killed by Damon, the demon. I was shocked, dazed, and in disbelief, although I knew he was capable. He shot her twice in the head. One bullet went through her hand as she was holding her hand over her face. And all while she had his baby girl, still in pampers, sitting right on the bed with her. I strongly advise any and every woman if you get in a relationship and the man gets physical with you, leave the first time and don't look back. Now once again my heart feels as if someone has stabbed me in the heart. I have to say I did see this one coming. He took her away from 5 girls and one being his own.

Chapter 38

Destroying the Demon That's Trying to Destroy Me

*K*illing the personal cocaine demon that I had entertained was next. Now that the in-house supplier was gone, I had to supply my own coc and weed by doing my own dealing. The bills were now all on me. One thing for sure I wasn't about to allow myself to become a woman who would sleep around with every man for drugs. I had seen too many women totally lose who they were in the drug scene. After the things Rod had told me about what had happened to so many women. I had determined I would rather be dead than to turn out to be that woman. It wasn't an option. I never have contemplated suicide, but I knew I'd rather be dead than allow myself to fall into that pit. Having made moves on my own before Greg. I knew I could do what I needed to do, buying and selling for myself until I got free of that demon. I began dating a younger guy that really stepped in to protect me from Greg and helped me through the process. I was crazy about this guy but so was another girl in the area, although I didn't know he had been in a relationship with her. I guess once my new guy realized Greg was out of the way, he wasn't giving the girl the attention she desired.

Apparently, she knew all about me. She had begun circulating vicious rumors about me and I didn't know why until I found out it was over the man. I had enough, one day I had decided I was going to her apartment door and take my pistol and beat her with it. Then before I could make the move to visit her, I had an Open Vision. I was standing at the sink in the kitchen when someone was at my front door shooting at me. The strange thing was that I noticed that as the shots reached me they turned to darts. They were stinging each time one hit me. Later, I found out that the Word of God warns us of the fiery darts of the devil, (Ephesians 6: 16). The front door was parallel to the kitchen sink. I turned to run toward the front door but then took a detour to my closet and grabbed my pistol and headed to the front door. Before I got to the front door the pistol fell from my hand. Every part of it scattered all over the carpet, the barrel, hammer, trigger, bullets and all hit the floor. Then I heard an audible voice speak loud and clear, "I'll Fight Your Battles For You." I replied, "Lord, Is That You?" Once again, He said, "I'll Fight Your Battles For You." I said, "Yes, Lord." Then I saw the guy I was seeing in the yard. I walked toward the front door. We smiled at each other and he waved goodbye. I continued outside and I could see a marketplace directly in front of my house. I walked to cross the street to go get some of the items. But as soon as my feet hit the pavement I looked up and there were three planets, and one was so big and close to me I reached up to touch it and I said, "Glory to God!!!" Then I looked across the street and I saw myself filling these baskets with all types of things, food, and every type of cleaning product you'd ever need. Then I came out of the vision.

Then I told God, "Ok I'm leaving it in your hands. I trust you." Within no time at all everything that the girl had rumored about me, I was hearing it was actually happening to her and much more. I learned then how to let God fight my battles when it comes to people. I promise you He can fight for you and you don't have to get your hands dirty. The full vision played out just as it was revealed. The guy and I went our separate ways on the best of terms and always remained good friends. I moved into a new environment and got my spiritual house clean and began giving God all the glory.

Once Greg realized that the relationship was definitely over, he became furious, threatening to burn me up in the house. Women, please, if a man threatens your life, take it seriously. After the many phone calls and belligerent conversations from Greg, I began to take what he said not as just talk, but threats that I couldn't take a chance on him making good on.

Remember there's a thin line between love and hate. One day he showed up unexpectedly and kicked in my door. I ran to the closet in my bedroom. He knew that that was the place where I kept my weapon. By the time I came out of the room with the weapon in my hand he was on his knees pleading with me not to shoot him but to take him back. He had been sneaking around my house to see what was going and who I had been seeing. He had also hung out at the telephone booth across the street at the store to monitor what was going on at my house. If at any time a man is stalking you, be prepared for anything. My mind was made up. There was no turning back.

Chapter 39

Slaying the Demon Within

For one year I struggled. The adjustment of moving forward was not necessarily easy, but it was much welcomed. I began to pray earnestly, asking God to step in. One night I dreamed of being in a new apartment. The place was so peaceful. There was a window to the left of the kitchen sink and a breeze that blew through the window facing the backyard. The apartment was immaculately clean. Soon after I went to visit my Mom. While there I visited my aunt and she made a suggestion that I should move near them. She suggested that I talk to a friend of hers about the availability of an apartment not far from her house. I reluctantly went to speak to the lady.

The apartment was available, and she would take me to look at it while I was there. Once I entered the apartment I was overcome by the feeling of familiarity. After entering the kitchen and dining area, I remembered the dream. The kitchen sink and window were located exactly as in the dream. The cleanliness and the peace resonated in the atmosphere. I felt as though I had just walked into the dream I had. Within a couple of weeks, I received a call informing me that I was approved for the apartment. The city of Birmingham was no longer going to be the place I called home. Sometimes God's plan for your deliverance is to move you away from the environment that you're in to one that is more conducive for your future productivity. Leaving behind what's familiar is sometimes the best thing that could happen to you. Don't fight the process.

Although I was happy about the transition, I was dealing with taking the drug demon along with me to the new place. I fought to resolve the problem, but it continued to follow. Even a new place won't make you new. You must be ready to become a new creature. So, for about a year I began attending church more and more. One night I went to buy some cocaine to sell and ended up using it all. I told my cousin who was with me that once we left the place, "That's it! I'm done. I'm never doing cocaine again." I meant it. I knew the answer was not in me but in the one that had brought me through so many trials and dangers seen and unseen. I made my mind up I was going to a church I heard about in Birmingham, where people were getting delivered and set free from strongholds of the enemy. I told God that I knew He could do it for me, and when that Wednesday came, I was coming through those doors for my deliverance. That Wednesday night, I entered those doors fully expecting deliverance because I had faith that God knew I meant business. He knew I believed He had a better plan for my life. He had delivered me from Greg, and now He would deliver me from myself. I entered the service. I can't tell you what was preached; my focus was on the altar call. When the pastor opened the church for an altar call, I went up looking to Jesus to touch me. The next thing I knew I was on the other side of the room, praising God in total rapture, feeling a fire, a heat, a presence of joy, face tore up, sweating, crying, hair, and makeup totally all over the place. No man had laid hands on me, not even gotten close to me. Just the Spirit of God. I was free and have been ever since, over thirty years. That following Friday I attended church asking

GOD to fill me with His Spirit. It didn't happen at church that night, but once I was home alone praying, I began speaking in my heavenly language. It was the most beautiful experience I had ever had next to holding my babies for the first time. The relationship with Christ was the one I needed to give all my attention to that day forward.

Chapter 40

Satan Has Desire to Sift You as Wheat

I started Cosmetology school while in Birmingham but I did not finish the course. My new city had a local Community College that offered the course. I wanted to own a Salon and Beauty Supply. Now that I was delivered from drugs, I needed to focus on a future to advance the well-being of my family.

In the process of focusing my attention on Christ, the Nigerian shows up in my life after being on hiatus for about five years. The ironic thing was that I was warned in a dream not to go back to dealing with him. It reminds me of Matthew 2:12 when the Wise Men were warned in a dream not to go back to Herod but to return to their country by another route. The problem was I wasn't as wise. I disobeyed the vision; I was shown in a dream that he was coming. In the dream, I saw him riding a bike, wearing jeans and a tee-shirt. I heard the voice of the Lord saying, "Have nothing to do with him." Shortly after he contacted us and wanted to visit his child. One thing leads to another. Just as I was warned in the dream. He showed up no longer driving the new luxury cars or the tailored suits. Now he is struggling. Working managing an Electronic Store. That was beneath him, but humble was not part of his character, which contributed to the quick resolution of our reconciliation. That was something I could have been spared from dealing with if I had obeyed the warning God had given me in the dream. I've learned if God goes to the trouble of warning you of something in a dream, be wise enough to take heed because it will not end well if you don't. We ended up having a big fallout within three months, which ended the relationship for me forever. Those three months cost me a setback for my disobedience. When I decided to get involved again with him, I had chosen a man over my relationship with God. Just that plain and simple. I was in what is called a backsliding state. Which simply means turning back to the old way of thinking. The Holy Spirit told me don't turn away. But when you engage in sexual activity, you open yourself to soul ties and emotional rollercoasters. It took me about two years to really get totally surrendered to God in that area after that foolish decision. Thinking a man was necessary took another deliverance and renewing of the mind. For two years I was in a backslidden state.

I started to date a guy that proposed to me. His mom didn't like me. Why? I wasn't quite sure. His mom started inviting his ex to her house daily and made sure I saw her because she lived down the street. Although he didn't live with his mom, he did live across the street from her. I told him he needed to nip in the bud what was going on with his mom and his ex. Since he couldn't get control of the situation, I gave the ring back and moved on. If a man can't put his ex in check and his mother about the woman, he claims he wants to marry, he still needs to stay single and entertain the both of them.

As soon as the word got around that the marriage was off, another guy was waiting in the wings. He was the brother of one of my cousin's boyfriend. I had known him for a while. He

Janet Evans

was a really fun guy who was older and wasn't wasting time either. In about six months he proposed, and we were at his family reunion and I was being introduced as his fiancé. A week later, I was summoned by his mother to come to her house for her to get to know the woman her son was marrying. Interestingly enough, after the meeting, when I got home, God began to speak to me. Telling me not to entangle myself because they looked to other gods. I invited the guy to attend church with me at a Prophet's Church. He didn't show up to go. I knew that I had to walk away even though it was what I wanted. I learned that what I want and what God wants for me can be totally opposite. And that I have had to choose God's way to my own hurt sometimes. Knowing He is always right. I can say I've never regretted it. It wasn't easy because I enjoyed the relationship and thought he was one I could be happy with. He couldn't understand why I changed my mind. When I told him, he didn't believe me. I told him I was going to go to church and surrender everything to God because I felt him calling me into a closer relationship with him. I said to him, "I'm going to church and I'm never coming back to the world's way of doing things." And so, I did. Often, I would see him driving by the church I attended to see if I was in attendance. After a year I guess he was convinced and understood I was committed.

I couldn't marry a man that wasn't interested in serving God. I knew it would be a disaster.

Chapter 41

Virtuous Woman

I decided I only needed to serve God and be alone with Him. That is what I did. It was the very best decision I ever made. I spent the next two years staying focused on my relationship with GOD, so that I could learn how to become that Virtuous Woman He called me to be. During my time alone with GOD, I realized I needed that time to really fall in love with HIM and fall in love with the woman I had become. I focused on renewing my mind according to the word and becoming a doer of what I heard. I began understanding the principles of GOD, understanding that if we followed His principles, our lives would be blessed. Being a Virtuous Woman is really the ability to unapologetically express the inward Phenomenal Woman that the Word of GOD is creating in you outwardly. The woman whose speech is tempered, handles her business, her house is well kept, as well as her family and herself. She honors GOD and works diligently with her husband building their home. If she is a single woman, she presents her body to GOD as a temple for Him to live in. Free from sexual impurity, foul language, and drunkenness. This is a challenge for everyone no matter how much you love the LORD. The flesh is always wanting to be given what makes it feel pleasure. I was doing all of this, and then after about two years, the guy I gave the ring back to and mother who didn't like me started showing up at church. Week after week, month after month, he attended church. Then one day, he went to the altar and committed his life to God.

We started dating again, only this time according to the Word of GOD, NO fornication. Look, you know as well as I do, you have to be under the influence of the Holy Spirit to keep the flesh under subjection to the Word of GOD. You have to set boundaries when it comes to dating. Then stick with them until you not only have a ring on it but can say, "I IS Married." He seemed so sincerely dedicated to GOD and the things of GOD. I thought for sure I had gotten my Knight and Shining Armor. Later I found myself cleaning up after the horse. The next thing I know we're planning a wedding. It was a beautiful wedding ceremony with my children and all our family and friends. Even his mom and I were on good terms after I requested a meeting with her to discuss our issue. The honeymoon in Vegas was wonderful. In two years we had a nice five-bedroom home, vacations and timeshares. He bought me a BMW and things seemed to be going well. Then God gives me a dream. The dream was our home looked spectacular from the outside, but the foundation was unstable and shaking. My husband stopped going to church and started hanging out with his old friends. Then one day God asked me what would you do if you found out your husband is cheating? I sat down on the steps going downstairs. I said, "Lord, I tell you what I'm not going to do is turn my back on you and go back to my old way of life." I felt betrayed, even tricked, because within a year's time he stopped serving God altogether. I prayed and fasted until I was looking like Olive-Oil. I must have had my concerns about the area of infidelity before I married him. Not because of anything I had caught him doing. I knew it ran rampant in his family. I also had discussed it with him before we married. I told him and GOD I would not stay in an unfaithful marriage. By our second year of marriage, I had gotten called of GOD into ministry. Initially my husband didn't have a problem with it when I told him. Yet within a couple of months, I was doing my first sermon; he refused to come. I was so shocked the evening of the service. He came in from work, showered and I assumed was getting dressed. When I came into the bedroom to say I was ready he was on the bed undressed informing me he wouldn't be attending. I really didn't see that coming. I was so hurt because we had always supported one another. I didn't have time to deal with the distraction because within the hour I was about to deliver my first message of GOD to the waiting congregation. The cross was heavy, but it was mine to bear. At that moment I was reminded of the vision GOD had given me a few years before when I stood at the ocean at night and the waves came crashing to shore. As I stood there feeling as insignificant as one of the grains of sand under my feet, that would be washed away with the next approaching wave. I heard the voice of GOD speak like thunder rolling over the water. "You Are Your Brother's Keeper." I replied, "Yes, LORD," and again, "You Are Your Brother's Keeper." I replied again once more, "Yes, LORD." HE then said, "Must JESUS bear the cross alone and all the world go free there's a cross for everyone." I then awoke out of the vision speaking out loud saying, "There's a cross for me." I believed the fact that the enemy was waging such warfare was the true indication of my calling. Soon after that sermon, the attacks began to increase.

The dream of me opening a Salon and Beauty Supply Store became a reality. I completed my courses and became a licensed Cosmetologist. I even made the Dean's List. GLORY TO GOD! Then I acquired my Managing License. My husband supported

Janet Evans

the vision fully, physically, and financially. Yet the Holy Spirit was revealing that he was cheating. Although I had no physical evidence to tie to it. I would warn him that the Holy Spirit said there was nothing hid that wouldn't be revealed and that warning comes before destruction. I tried to save my marriage, but you can't save a marriage any more than you can a person that doesn't want to be saved. I had promised him before marrying him that I wouldn't tolerate cheating. No matter what we may have accomplished together I would end the marriage. He continued trying to buy things and take me on trips.

For our seventh wedding anniversary we went to Miami for a week. I knew when we got there that the marriage was over. I prayed for God to let me catch him without excuse and when I did, I knew I was rightfully free. One year I walked into a local Supermarket at Valentine. There on display was a giant basket, full of what I thought was a surprisingly good selection of items. Of course, candy and bear. I remember looking at the price, thinking some young girl would really be impressed to receive it and even some women. A couple of days later the husband comes in from work and goes to shower leaving his dirty cloth in the bedroom on the floor. Normally I would not have paid that much attention. Only this time I heard the HOLY Spirit say get his wallet out. I said, "I don't need any of his money." He said again, "Look in the wallet." As soon as I pulled the wallet out, I saw a Wire Receipt and a purchase for the exact amount of the Giant Valentine basket, and it listed the item as a holiday gift. I took the receipts and stuck the wallet back in his pocket. Not mentioning to him anything about it at that time. I was definitely under the influence of the Holy Spirit. The next day I used the tracking number on the Wire Receipt to call to ask if the package had been delivered to the correct address. From that I was able to get the name of the person to whom it was sent.

The funny thing was even after I had all the information, the Lord would not allow me to say anything. He instructed me to do something that my flesh loathed. Which was to go through with the plan for a romantic Valentine Night away. I was being challenged to do something I had NO desire to do. I obeyed. After getting to our destination, I thought for sure I wouldn't have to go through with the facade. Honestly, I thought once we were all comfy with the romantic atmosphere set, I would put the receipts I'd found in the card along with thanks for the gift basket and sign her name. Yet the Holy Spirit said "NO! Hold your peace." I was so NOT willing, but I forced myself to obey. I suffered through the fake romantic night. It was truly one of the most difficult tasks for me. That's what it means to die to self. Maybe someone reading this can relate to being in a marriage where love making is more of a chore than a pleasure.

For me knowing that he was cheating only caused my desire for him to become non-existent. It was as if everything about him was offensive. I couldn't explain it, other than it was like sheep and goats. The breath of a goat is so offensive. Sheep and goat rarely ever mate. Even though they can graze in the same area, mating is not common. When they do, it produces "geep." A species that life span is extremely short, such was our marriage, compared to it supposedly lasting a lifetime. Some days it took every fiber of my being not to do something other than what the LORD required of me. I held my peace. Shortly after the husband informed me he was planning to go to Philadelphia to visit his cousin. They were going to get together with another friend from our town that had moved there. I didn't need to go because they would be at the casinos. I said, ok go ahead and enjoy your visit, but then I felt the release to confront him. As soon as he called to say he had arrived. I told him to make sure he said hello to everyone, especially the woman (Lyn-

Janet Evans

da) in Watertown, and to let me know if she liked the Valentine's gift basket that was delivered to her, then I gave him the address. He was shocked. Of course, he said she was a cousin, and he was sending it to her kids. I said I had already asked his mom if she knew Lynda Mason. She said no she didn't know her. So that took all the fun out of that visit. That was the first time I had tangible evidence. I felt I needed to try to at least give him another chance to straighten up. I would be lying if I said being in the Ministry didn't play a huge role in me staying longer. I thought I needed to fight the enemy that was coming against our marriage. Yes, I was hurt and angry, yet I knew I needed to at least give it my best before I walked away. So, I took on more prayer and fasting. I was trying to encourage him to return to GOD, but instead he turned a deaf ear. I honestly can say I started to resent him. I wanted the man that I thought I was marrying. The one who went to church, read his Bible and served over the church finances. I felt that Satan had hoodwinked and bamboozled me. I was sleeping with the enemy.

One night as we were in bed, he was asleep, and I saw this spirit of a woman come out of a dumpster looking filthy dirty, just foul. I discerned she was a prostitute, I said, "Get out of my house," but she continued to enter the room. She said, "NO!" I said again, "GET OUT!" She said, "NO, I was invited here." I said, "NO! You leave my house NOW by the Blood of JESUS and the Authority of HIS Name." She then began shrinking and finally disappeared. I then reached over and woke him up, telling him I was tired of warring in the spirit with the spirit of perversions that he was inviting in. He needed to get cleaned up, or someone would have to leave. Then after a short time I heard he was involved with a local stripper. Of course, by now my, long suffering was just about as short as it could get. I am now looking for the next opportunity to lay down a burden of proof, so I can kick him out. So, I agreed with a friend who felt her husband was up to the same kind of dirty deeds. If either of us saw one of our husbands with another woman, we would say so. Shortly after my father-in-law passed, maybe a week after a family celebration at his house, I had gone by the gathering. When I arrived, there was a crowd. The family is so large when you add friends and cousins, you have a block-party. For some reason, there was this one female that just stood out to me. She was with one of the nephews' girlfriends. So, I asked the husband, "Who is that girl with our niece?" His reply was, "I don't know; she came with our nephew's girlfriend." Yet the Holy Spirit put a check in my Spirit, saying no there's more to it. Knowing that I never stayed long at any of the gatherings, he put on a big show about his wife this and that. After thirty minutes I left the scene, leaving them to their party. As I stated earlier my father-in -law passed away the next week. I went to my friend's house that I had made a pact with to check on getting my hair done. Once I got there, she was acting a little uncomfortable. She asked how my husband was doing? I told her that he was doing ok, but he was at his dad's house with his mother. He told me that he may stay the night with her just to keep her company. My friend looked puzzled. She asked me if I was ok with that? I said yea, he can stay. I said, "Tell me what you're getting at." She said, "Remember our pact? I really didn't want to tell you this, but my kids have come home over the last weeks asking why your husband is hanging out at my cousin's house with my cousin from California." She said she definitely didn't want me to find out about it and know that the woman was her cousin.

Thinking she was hiding it because they were kin. I was really cool. I called the husband and told him I would be pulling up outside his mom's house in a few minutes. I asked him to come outside. When he came to the car, I asked him who Karen was; again, he's looking like a deer caught in headlights. I said, "You know the woman I asked you about last week, that you didn't know her or her name. The one you've been hanging out with." I then told him I was glad that he was staying with his Mom, because I was done with his cheating and lying. He could come get his things and go wherever he wanted. Little did he know he was not only about to mourn the loss of his father but also his marriage.

He tried to come home and sleep in the bed, saying I couldn't put him out of his house. By then I had shifted into another frame of mind -the place where I was warring not just with him but with my flesh and the devil. I told him if he thought he could just lay down in that bed and sleep without waking up to something he deserved, then stay. He stayed that night, but I don't think he slept. Of course, I had moved into the other bedroom anyway. After that, he went to stay at his mom's. He called every day wanting to come home. I refused his calls for at least two weeks. Then I wanted the real truth. So, I told him I would talk only if he was willing to tell the truth. He agreed. As we stood in the kitchen, I got him to tell me all about him meeting Karen. His story conveniently was told short of him sleeping with her. By now I didn't care one way or the other. What I really wanted to know about was who I suspected he was seeing while working in Birmingham. So, I lured him into telling me the truth that he was seeing someone while he was working there. I wanted to know what side of town she lived on, because the job site was located in Fairfield, my hometown. He could have said any other part of Birmingham, but he didn't. When he said Fairfield, I didn't curse him out, I never did. I was holding a cast iron skillet. I drew back and swung to strike him. YES, the virtuous preacher woman had let anger override the HOLY SPIRIT in her. The man jumped to escape the direct hit to his head. Running through the den and living room to escape through the front door. While I stood there angry that the handle on the cast iron skillet had broken when I hit him, I realized that I could have killed the man if I had made direct contact with his head instead of his shoulder and upper thigh since he was sitting on the steps. I already knew the marriage was over but the truth of just how unfaithful he had been was just being uncovered. I went upstairs and fell prostrate before the LORD and cried out for HIM to deliver me from anger. I knew how close I had come to doing irreversible damage, deadly boldly harm. I was so afraid, not of him, but myself. I was not crying for the marriage. I was hurt for the way I allowed the enemy to provoke me. I thought what if the next day's News headlines would have read ``Preacher Kills Estranged Husband bashing his head with cast iron skillet." Not a good testimony. I still continued to hold on to my relationship with God. I cried out to God and he delivered me. I was so hurt. After all, I had given my life to GOD, trying to do things the right way, even answered the call to ministry, I had been faithful to God and to my husband.

Nevertheless, I had to forgive and move on with life. I believed I had the perfect grounds for divorce. I went and paid for it thinking we would have no problem resolving the issue. We were married 10 years before it finally dissolved. My ex-husband had hurt me worse than I'd ever been hurt in a relationship. I still had to forgive him to move on. I resolved our partnership in the Beauty Supply and Salon business and divided the other properties we had attained. I trusted GOD to sustain me. Started working again in the Lab and did hair on weekends. I struggled financially and emotionally for a while. Sometimes you will have to suffer something in life. No one is exempt, but it is better to suffer for righteousness. I can say I made the right decision and have never regretted it. Why? Because God has shown himself strong on my behalf over and over again. God will take care of you.

Chapter 42

Danger Seen and Unseen

I'll never forget one day I was sitting at work, looking out the window when I had a Day vision. My thoughts were on a procedure I was having in the next few days. Ladies, please take care of your body. Do self-breast exams and your mammograms. I had found a lump and was getting a biopsy. As I looked out the window, I could see myself lying on a table. The doctors were doing the procedure but had made a terrible mistake. He had gone deep into the chest wall and punctured my heart, causing blood to spurt out like water from a pressure washer. I began to pray right then and there against that happening. Asking the Lord to shield me with His Hand, His Spirit, and send His Angels before me. When I showed up for my procedure, they put me in a gown, then on the table. They had all the instruments on the cart next to the table. There were two nurses, and they talked about what to expect and getting started shortly. For some reason, they kept going in and out of the room. One and then the other, although the doctor never showed up. Finally, one of the nurses came back in and said, "I'm sorry and honestly embarrassed to tell you this. The physician who was supposed to do this biopsy says he is not comfortable using this instrument and has declined to do your procedure." "WHAT!" I jumped off that table so fast with that surgical gown flying in the wind, trying to get out of the room. The nurse said, "Ms. Evans hold on. Would you like to reschedule, and don't you want to put your clothes on?" "No! No! I just need to get out of here." I ran around the room, grabbing my cloth halfway putting them on. I just need to tell of the faithfulness of God. He had just stepped in and touched that doctor's heart. God caused him to humble himself and admit he didn't know what he was doing with an instrument, which would have caused my death or irreparable damage.

Another lesson, If God shows you something, it's for you to pray for it or against it. For it to be loosed or bound in Heaven and in Earth. In Jesus Name. Matthew 18:18, "Whatever you bind on earth is already bound in heaven, and whatever you loose on earth it shall be loosed in heaven."

Chapter 43

Remaining Virtuous Dating After Divorce

I didn't date at all for four years after the divorce. I was healing and the time was absolutely needed. The ministry work was opening up, doors were opening in every direction. I traveled so much in one year, I didn't want to get on another plane or boat by the end of the year. The 24-hour flight to Nairobi, Kenya, was exhausting but incredible. The ministry work there was a big success and was very fruitful. I was busy serving GOD. He had enlarged my territory from North, East, South, West, and Overseas. As God poured out favor on my life, my pain and brokenness became a faint memory. The joy of the LORD was healing and strength.

Then I came across my first possible male interest. He was a divorcee with two kids, a Deacon at his church, and a hard worker. We went out for a while, but we were definitely on two different levels of commitment when it came to presenting our bodies to the LORD. My flesh was at war with my spirit so bad I literally came home laid prostrate on the floor crying out to GOD to deliver me. The battle to live Holy was on. I wanted the man, the company, the attention, the fellowship, and the future we talked about -the house he wanted to buy with a VA loan and move me to this new nearby subdivision. I just wasn't

Janet Evans

willing to compromise the relationship with God to satisfy my flesh or his before marriage. No, I'm not for sale nor a prostitute.

Let me just pause for a moment: You may be saying she is always talking about what a man buys her. Some of you women reading this book may need to be renewed in your mind through the Word of GOD. I am not a buyer or seller of love because it is not love if it can be bought or sold. Yet some of you may need to read EZEKIEL 16: 30-34, where GOD talks about women who are worse than a prostitute, being so eager to have a man that you have not demanded payment. He says, "Unlike the prostitutes that charge for their services, but not you. You give gifts and rewards to all your lovers bribing them to have sex with you." That is why some men are ruined. He doesn't have to keep a job, pay his own bills because he can squat at your place and drive your car. Then you got the nerve to call another woman a gold digger. Yes, there are some, but that's for another topic of discussion. Now, let me get back to me obeying GOD.

Then GOD began to say, "Cut It." I wanted to, but I kept playing around with it. Then GOD showed me a rope and a pair of scissors, the scissors cut the rope into. One piece remained in the hand and the other piece fell to the ground. Then GOD said, "Just like this rope there is NO longer any connection." I could clearly see GOD meant business. I had to choose one or the other, because I was playing with fire. God said, "Don't shake hands with your friend lucifer." When I told the guy that I wasn't going to be spending any time with him, he said, "Well, let's just shake hands and remain friends." He reached out his hand to shake my hand. I snatched my hand back so quickly. He said, "What's wrong? Can't we just shake hands?" He had no idea what that meant to me. I felt it would have been making a covenant agreement with the devil. I walked away and stopped answering his calls. Warning Comes Before Destruction. You know when you're being drawn away by your own lust. I refused and left running like Joseph from Potiphar's wife in Genesis, the 39th chapter. If I was going to preach Holy living, I would have to live what I preached.

I escaped only by the grace of GOD. I had danced around the fire with gasoline drawers too many times with this guy. I pleaded with GOD not to let me catch on fire. Flesh is flesh and is always warring against the Spirit of God. Through my obedience, I "Cut It" and made it through the fiery trial. That's why 1 Corinthians 10:13 (NLV), it says, "The temptations in your life are no different from what others experience. And God is faithful. He will not allow the temptation to be more than you can stand." When you are tempted, He will show you a way out so that you can endure. Being a Virtuous Woman is serious business. GOD promised us He would give us all things that pertain to life and Godliness (2 Peter 1:3).

Then there was the one guy that showed up checking everything on my list. He was saved, loved God, of course, single but widowed, no children. He liked outreach evangelist work, feeding the homeless, providing clothes to the needy, and traveling. He wasn't afraid to fly and had his own money. I figured a man who had been married would have had enough experience in knowing how marriage works. Not only did I think he was the one, so did my close friend that knew what my checklist included. When she met him, she said, "Girl, I got chills; I think he's the one." He was respectful, hardworking, fun loving, and loved family. We had so much in common that kept us working together on projects. I had a radio program that aired on Sunday mornings. He was my biggest sponsor. I had written a stage play; he was a sound and light guy and had committed to the project. He was a musician. When I needed one for a surprise birthday party for my mom, he was there. We became the best of friends. People began to spread rumors. I had a house built and it was said that he lived with me. Some said I had married him. As a minister, you do care about your reputation, but you can't let everything people say (behind your back) order your life especially when it's a lie.

The downside to our relationship was, he and I had denominational differences that were very challenging. The reality of the differences became the apparent deal breaker for me. Although we loved each other dearly, it was evident, being a couple was not where we were headed. I could appreciate that we were honest enough to understand that sometimes love is not always enough. Sometimes a person has another purpose in your life than Eros love. Which was the case with Wil and me. Everyone was rooting for us to become husband and wife. Fortunately for me, I saw early on that it was not what it was to be. Even though I moved on he continued to treat me so good. I asked him why and he said that GOD told him to, and he promised he would. He would show up early in the morning park in my driveway sometimes before I got up, waiting to drop off all types of gifts for me or my grandkids. Sometimes unbeknown to me, was outside for hours without disturbing me because he could hear me praying. I guess if I was on the outside looking in, I would have thought this man must be sleeping with this woman the way he constantly cares for her.

Then one day he came by and during our conversation, he said to me, "I told you I promised GOD I'd take care of you. But now I'm going to have to give you to your Apostle.'" I said, "What are you talking about? That man ain't studying me. Laughingly I said, No, no, a promise is a promise." Our visits became a lot less frequent once or twice a month, meeting for dinner with my granddaughter; he was her godfather. I went to Jamaica in December for Christmas, when I came back, I saw him in January around my birthday. Before his birthday in March, he passed away from a massive heart attack. I thought no wonder he was giving me to a spiritual leader. His assignment was over. My heart was so wounded from the loss. GOD had allowed him to be taken without any time for goodbyes. The one thing that gave me great comfort and joy was, he told me I had really shown him what a real Christian Woman was… one that really prayed and was Virtuous.

I was so thankful to have passed the test of not luring this man into a sexual relationship that could have caused him to lose his soul. No wonder the bible says a Virtuous Woman's price is far above rubies because a man really knows the value of a Virtuous Woman.

I just wish more women knew their worth.

Listen, God is the best Father you could ever have. He continues to provide, open doors, and fulfill many dreams. I've been blessed to preach on radio and television to women who are broken and desire to live a life that glorifies GOD. A life still filled with excitement, adventure, and fun. Even if you desire to be a wife and your husband has not found you, you should be living your best life. All while you are yearning to discover your reason for being on this planet and fulfilling your purpose? All while unearthing the Virtuous Woman inside.

Serving God has caused me to be the best me that I can be. I can say I Love, Love "The life" in Christ Jesus that I live.

Janet Evans

It's a wonderful journey being a Virtuous Woman!

AUTHOR JANET EVANS

THE END

Janet Evans

About the Author

Janet Evans is from Birmingham, Alabama. She has three children and is a grandmother to four grandchildren. Janet is an Ordained Evangelist and Elder. She has traveled continuously to serve and share the truth of the KINGDOM Of GOD. She has worked in both radio and television ministry encouraging women to thrive in life.